Better to Die
The Story of the
Gurkhas

By the same author :

THE WOODEN WONDER
THE BATTLE OF BRITAIN
BLOOD AND FIRE!
EMMA, LADY HAMILTON
WELLINGTON BOMBER
THEIR FINEST HOUR
THE GUINEA PIG CLUB
THE DEBT WE OWE

Better to Die

The Story of the
Gurkhas

EDWARD BISHOP

NEW ENGLISH LIBRARY
TIMES MIRROR

Contents

'Kafar hunne bhanda morno ramro'
('Better to die than be coward')

List of Illustrations

PLATES   *Between pages 64–65*

Sir David Ochterlony *(Radio Times Hulton Picture Library)*

Field-Marshal Lord Roberts *(Radio Times Hulton Picture Library)*

Karanbahadur Rana, First World War VC *(Photographers International)*

Rifleman of the 1/2nd Gurkhas *(Imperial War Museum)*

General Montgomery with Gurkhas in Africa *(Imperial War Museum)*

Riflemen of the 1/2nd Gurkhas, charging *(Imperial War Museum)*

Captain Michael Allmand VC *(Imperial War Museum)*

Rifleman Tulbahadur Pun VC *(Imperial War Museum)*

Lieutenant-General Slim *(Imperial War Museum)*

A Gurkha in action against the Japanese *(Imperial War Museum)*

A Gurkha in action in Burma *(Imperial War Museum)*

Gurkhas and Grenadier Guards on parade *(Photographers International)*

MAPS

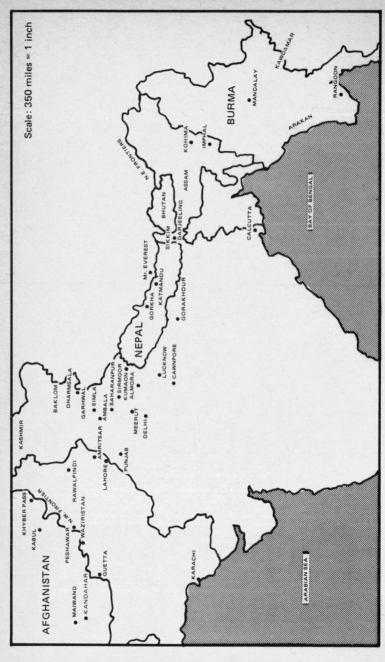

Figure 1 India and its frontiers

CHAPTER ONE

The Nepal War, 1814–16

Visitors to London are occasionally mystified to observe that the tall British sentries in scarlet tunics and bearskin caps usually to be found outside Buckingham Palace have been replaced by short Asians wearing rifle-green and flat slouch hats set at a jaunty angle. The nearest policeman will tell them that sometimes the honour of guarding the Queen's official residence passes from the Brigade of Guards to units of the Gurkha Rifles, which are recruited from Nepal to serve in the British Army. A youthful police-man's knowledge might not take him beyond this explanation, but some old soldiers could add that regiments of Gurkhas have been serving the Crown, and fighting alongside British troops, since a far-off and obscure war of more than 160 years ago which led to the recruitment of hillmen from Nepal.

The origins of the Nepal War of 1814–16 were bizarre even by early nineteenth-century standards. The war was entered into by an Irish soldier who, much in debt, had been appointed Governor-General of India through the influence of his friend the Prince Regent, a post which, offering £25,000 a year, it was hoped would assist him to restore his financial stability. Thereafter, the war was largely paid for by an Indian potentate who saw in it an opportunity to extend his power.

The Irishman who went to war with the Gurkhas,
Francis Rawdon-Hastings, 2nd Earl of Moira and 1st
Marquess of Hastings—he was thus ennobled following
the Nepal War—had arrived in India at the age of fifty-
nine after a very mixed career as soldier, rake, gambler,
politician and go-between for the Prince Regent with his
mistresses. It was a controversial appointment, for it was
on record that Moira held the opinion that British government in India was founded on injustice.

Katmandu for Christmas. The prospect of dropping such
a seasonable gift as the centre of Gurkha power in Nepal
into the Honourable East India Company's stocking appealed to Lord Moira who, as he prepared for war in
November 1814, was confident that 30,000 British and
Indian troops, 12,000 native auxiliaries, 60 guns, 1,113
elephants and 3,682 camels would swiftly overwhelm the
Gurkhas. Moreover, he could congratulate himself that the
ruler of Oudh had been persuaded to pay expenses against
promises of territorial gain and that the Raja of Tirhout
had agreed to provide 473 of the elephants.

The confidence of this tall, athletic Irishman, a stately
and impressive figure who, despite his dissolute past, had
retained a strong physique, is excusable. From all accounts
the Gurkhas were a primitive, poorly armed, little organised people, solely protected by a border belt of fever-
ridden jungle known as the Terai, and by difficult mountain
country. Militarily Moira, who had embarked at Ports-
mouth on 14 April 1813 and arrived at Calcutta in early
October, was as experienced as any of his subordinates in
the East. There was the difference, however, that he had
soldiered with European troops in the West, collecting two
bullet-holes in his cap at Bunker Hill during the American
War of Independence before taking part in the Battles of
Brooklyn and White Plains and raising a corps at

Philadelphia known as the Volunteers of Ireland.

Invasion on the scale planned by Moira required preparation and a measure of authority from the East India Company's court of directors in London. Moira's decision to march against the Gurkhas was not, therefore, the impulsive gesture of a freshly appointed governor-general, but the outcome of a long series of irritations returning to the period of his predecessor, the Earl of Minto. The Gurkhas of Nepal had been reported to London in official papers as 'insolent' and 'aggressive' since British India had first rubbed up against their frontiers as a result of Oudh's cession in 1801 of territory around Gorakhpur to the East India Company. Beginning as pinprick border incidents these aggressions had graduated into raids, culminating in the murder on 29 May 1814 of eighteen police at three British frontier-posts in Butwal. Provocation of this gravity was unacceptable, and while the court of directors in London might, given time, have preferred to veto such total reprisal as war, early nineteenth-century communications ruled out day-to-day instant consultation, a factor which left Moira free to launch a full-scale punitive campaign with little further ado.

In Katmandu the Gurkha leadership felt equally provoked, and no one more so than Bhim Sen Thapa, Nepal's powerful prime minister, who regarded the British intrusion of his territory as a threat to national security and no less to his personal fortune. The East India Company's frontier police, as with those slain in Butwal, had moved into villages from which members of Bhim Sen's family drew considerable revenue, never mind that in reality the East India Company was more concerned with consolidation than expansion. The failure of Lord Minto's administration to react punitively to Gurkha pinpricks had been misinterpreted by Bhim Sen as British weakness and fear, and he rejected Lord Moira's proposals for a negotiated frontier settlement, discarding the advice of

Amar Singh Thapa, his commander-in-chief, to cede certain disputed villages to British India. He took the view that China had previously failed to overrun Nepal and that the British would stand as little if not less chance of penetrating its hills and fastnesses.

Amar Singh, for all Nepal's isolation, was a soldier whose military qualities were a match for those of Moira or of his generals. He had subjected the three neighbouring rajadoms of Sirmoor, Garhwal and Kumaon, some 400 miles west of Katmandu, and was military governor of these provinces and elsewhere in an area annexed by Gurkha force of arms. Conquest in the west had brought him into the vicinity of British forces commanded by a Colonel David Ochterlony, a hard soldier whose career had already earned him a reputation as 'the terrible Lony Ochter'. Indeed, wary of this one man, Amar Singh had considered it imprudent to venture further towards the boundaries of the East India Company's military power and political influence, and he cautioned the Gurkha Council in Katmandu by letter: 'We have hitherto but hunted deer. If we engage in this war we must prepare to fight tigers. The advocate of war who proposes to fight and conquer the English has been bred up at court and is a stranger to the toil and hardships of military life.'

Bhim Sen's refusal to give way meant, in the imperious view of a Victorian writer, that 'war became inevitable' and consequently 'an army was ordered to take the field in the autumn of that year', the frontier region of the disputed villages being considered too unhealthy out of the cold season.

Intelligence was scarce about Gurkha measures for the defence of Nepal and about the military capability of the defenders. Gurkhas were regarded as troublesome tribesmen to be taught their place behind a frontier and, possibly, subjugated by British India. Lord Moira thought it would all be over by Christmas. In the event his invading columns

encountered so much misfortune at the hands of the
Gurkhas that, quite apart from the Nepalese conflict being
obscured by Waterloo and other momentous events in
Europe of the period, written reference to it was dis-
couraged over the next hundred years for fear of alerting
the British Empire's subject peoples to the fallibility of
British soldiers and their arms. As recently as 1929 a
military historian, avoiding the issue, commented that the
operations of Moira's columns redounded 'so little to our
credit that the less said about them the better'. The fact
is that Gurkhas were redoubtable fighting men before
British officers laced hard ammunition-boots on to their
nimble mountain feet, drilled them on squares, inspired
them with Scottish pipe music and led them in some of
the bloodiest actions of Britain's wars. Moreover, they were
supported in the field by an organisation of sorts which,
if primitive, suited—as Bhim Sen recognised that it
would—the nature of a defensive war against invaders of
their country. Each soldier enjoyed the luxury of at least
one woman slave and a boy or two to carry provisions and
clothing and to do the cooking. This was an ideal system
for combating European invaders who required one camel
to carry the impedimenta of every eight soldiers; and it
freed men who were professional warriors to give themselves single-mindedly to soldiering.

Gurkha military professionalism extended to a readiness
to wear their Hindu religion lightly, and Moira's com-
manders were to envy their speed on the march and the
manoeuvrability to which it contributed. Whereas British-
employed Hindu troops were obliged to undress and wash
before meals, the Gurkhas merely removed head coverings
and made do with a face-and-hands cat-lick. Nor was
Nepal's regular army of up to 8,500, with as many reservists
on call, undisciplined. Before the Nepal War British
deserters had unintentionally prepared the way for subsequent Gurkha familiarity with and respect for British

words of command by drilling the army in British fashion at Katmandu. They had also instilled the Gurkhas with an appreciation of British military music, teaching one of their bands to play a selection of marching airs, including 'The Lass of Richmond Hill'. Bhim Sen's regulars mimicked the British Army to the extent of wearing scarlet jackets with white crossbelts, the officers adorning themselves as best they could in an imitation of frog-laced full dress, the most junior among them aspiring to resemble generals.

Katmandu for Christmas. Moira, taking a directly opposite view to Bhim Sen, was convinced that in mountain operations the difficulties would be greater for the defenders of Nepal than for his better equipped army and was confident of victory. He had paused since the murders in May for the rainy season to pass and now he marched four columns against Nepal. The plan was for two columns to defeat Amar Singh Thapa 400 miles west of Katmandu while two more columns converged on Katmandu itself in the east, the western and eastern operations being geographically separated by the Kali River. It was to be a walk-over, Moira excusing himself from accompanying the expedition on the ground that he might appear to be taking advantage of an easy opportunity to win personal glory. Writing off the Gurkhas before one elephant or camel of his considerable army had entered Nepal, he entrusted each column to the general who happened to command in the district where it was being assembled.

It was not long, however, before the unwisdom of this policy revealed itself in the experiences of the two columns ordered to operate east of the Kali. Setting out from Dinapore and Benares Major-Generals Bennet Marley and John Sulivan Wood were thrown back ignominiously. Entering the low, swampy, treacherous Terai and sweating up the foothills of Nepal the British and Indian troops of these two columns were repulsed by inferior numbers of Gurkhas wielding sticks and hurling stones. Some were pursued by the enemy 'sword in hand and driven for miles like a flock of sheep'. Although numbers were over-whelmingly to their advantage, the invaders admitted that bravery was on the side of the enemy. Very soon the elderly Commanders Marley and Wood had had enough of fighting Gurkhas, particularly Marley who, making off on horseback after dark, left his column to fare for itself. At this time he was sixty-one, yet he was to soldier on in India in obscurity, eventually being promoted full general at the age of eighty-five. However, in this odd and remote war, British military leaders held no monopoly of the bizarre. A heavily outnumbered Gurkha commander, who disobeyed orders to attack, was court-martialled at Katmandu and publicly paraded in petticoats.

Moira's western columns of 4,500 and 6,000 men fared better than had the eastern ones. This was partly because of the personalities and leadership qualities of their com-manders, Major-General Robert Rollo Gillespie and 'the terrible Lony Ochter', now also a major-general. Gillespie, aiming to enter Garhwal, marched from Saharanpur into Dehra Dun, only to find himself blocked from keeping a promise to link up with Ochterlony by a Gurkha garrison of less than 600 men in the hill fortress of Kalunga. Here, for the first time, were all the ingredients of the type of situation in which Gurkhas were to acquit themselves so courageously once they had entered British service.

In the last days of October 1814 Bal Bahadur Singh, the Gurkha garrison commander, looked down from the watch-tower of his rickety wood-and-stone stockade. In this wilderness, teeming with tiger and elephant, 4,000 men on the march, with 20 pieces of artillery stirring the dust on the route leading to Dehra Dun, presented a formidable enemy force. Nevertheless, on receiving written terms for surrender after dark, Bal Bahadur destroyed the offer

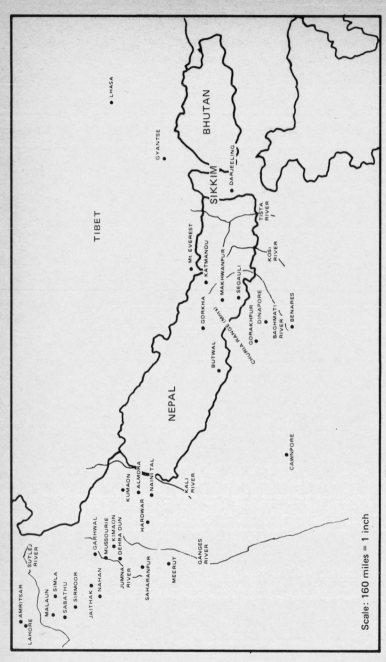

Figure 2   Nepal and the neighbouring states

Scale: 160 miles = 1 inch

contemptuously, commenting that he did not accept letters at such a late hour.

If Marley and Wood could be faulted for their timidity in the face of Gurkhas, Gillespie erred in the opposite extreme. An irascible Irish officer of His Majesty's 25th Dragoons, unloved in the column by reason of his harshness and uncompromising nature, he stood before Kalunga with a lifetime of scandal and no less courage to influence his decision-making. He was the man of action who, eight years earlier in his late thirties, had relieved, almost single-handed, the European survivors of a mutiny at Vellore near his command at Arcot. He was also, at this moment, the subject of allegations concerning seizure of young virgins for his personal satisfaction during recent service in Java. There were allegations against him, too, of insubordination and corruption in Java, and suggestions that head-wounds and excessive drinking had rendered him insane. Now at Kalunga, obsessed that fresh fame would clear the air of the various accusations being made against him in the Governor-General's circle at Calcutta, Gillespie, impatient for a quick and impressive victory, was enraged when a first assault by British and Indian troops was repelled by the Gurkha defenders. Survivors struggled back with reports of many being chopped down by a hook-like knife, possibly an agricultural implement. In their ignorance, those who had not previously encountered it were describing the broad, curved blade of the national weapon of Nepal which the British Army Gurkhas carry to this day–the kukri. It was excusable for Gillespie's men to suggest that they had been attacked with a farm implement because then, as now, the kukri was put to many purposes, from cutting up food for the pot to tree-felling and slaughtering goats. Gurkhas were even known to stake the left hand in a wager and cut it off with a kukri when they lost.

Gillespie, however, could not conceive the possibility of defeat by men who, as he saw it, were so primitively armed.

He led a fresh attack which fared no better and then, swearing that he would take the position or die in the attempt, led a party of dismounted Royal Irish Dragoons in a frontal assault. Shouting and brandishing his sword he ran head-on into musket-fire and was brought down 30 yards from the palisade. Beside him as he was killed was a certain Lieutenant Frederick Young, who was soon to figure in an historic incident which helped to hasten the regular recruitment of Gurkhas into British service.

This assault on the entrance to Kalunga left it intact, and now the column had to pause three weeks for the arrival of sufficient siege artillery and infantry reinforcements to sustain a fresh effort. In four days of bombardment at the end of November the invaders, assailed by musket-fire, arrows and stones from the fort, lost 36 dead and more than 430 wounded at the hands of a few hundred poorly equipped defenders.

The morale of the British and Indian troops was not improved by Bal Bahadur's return to them of the mutilated bodies of some of their fallen comrades. However, by nightfall on 29 November the sustained artillery-fire at last brought victory to Gillespie's column. With drums beating and stepping carefully between the dead and the dying, the British marched into the Gurkha stronghold in the early hours of the following morning.

But the drumbeat faltered as dawn revealed the full horror of the scene. Body lay across body and, intermingled with the dead, the wounded and the dying, women among them, groaned for water. Among the few of Bal Bahadur's men who had survived to retreat with their commander was Singhbir Thapa, a Gurkha boy who, more than forty years afterwards, was to be decorated with the Order of British India, an award for long and faithful service.

Kalunga had been overcome at heavy cost and although Gillespie's successor, Major-General Gabriel Martindell, another lacklustre general in the Marley mould, failed to exploit the victory, it was to contribute towards the severance of communications between the Gurkha-conquered dominion of Sirmoor, Garhwal and Kumaon in the west and Katmandu in the east. In the far west of this theatre, Ochterlony's column, some 6,000 strong and comprised entirely of native troops, was more successful than the rest of Moira's army. Here at the extremity of the East India Company's territory, some 400 miles west of Katmandu, Ochterlony, a seasoned campaigner who had lost an eye as a lieutenant in the Carnatic, was edging towards Amar Singh Thapa's fortress at Malaun. Between Ochterlony and Martindell another Gurkha force stood at Nahan, but fearing that it might be trapped, Amar Singh withdrew it to the hill fort of Jaithak.

Martindell moved against Jaithak, but without much enthusiasm. The fort lay behind a series of defended posts and villages which had first to be overrun, and the major-general, after losing one-third of his men before reaching the fort, opted for siege rather than assault. He hoped to starve out the garrison.

Ochterlony, meanwhile, had encountered similar ridge-by-ridge resistance and had met his own Kalunga at the peak of Deothal where 2,000 Gurkhas made an impassioned attempt to regain the position, 500 dying in battle. Ochterlony's success obliged Amar Singh to ask for terms from the fort at Malaun, to which, plagued by desertions, he had retreated with his remaining 200 men. The Jaithak garrison also sought terms. Ochterlony had succeeded where the leaders of Moira's three other columns had failed and it was not lost on the Governor-General that Ochterlony's division was the odd one out, in that it contained no European troops to stiffen the native regiments. Already the seeds of an idea were germinating: if Bengal sepoys could make some impact on such obviously re-doubtable fighting men as the Gurkhas of Nepal, then what could Gurkhas not achieve under British arms and leadership? Indeed, Ochterlony had already received sympathetic reaction from Lord Moira's staff to his advocacy of enlisting Gurkhas, and Gurkhas from surrendered positions were already marching under his orders before the end of the campaign in 1814.

Admiration of Gurkha bravery was reflected in Ochterlony's terms. Both Amar Singh at Malaun and his son, Ranjur Singh, at Jaithak were permitted to march out with arms and colours. Territorially Nepal was required to give up the Terai, the western districts of Kumaon, Garhwal and Sirmoor, and parts of neighbouring Sikkim. Diplomatically, Nepal had to accept the face-losing presence of a British resident in Katmandu. But Katmandu, far distant from Ochterlony's successes in the west, had not been imperilled by Moira's eastern columns and Bhim Sen refused to ratify the terms which Amar Singh had accepted at Malaun. News that the East India Company faced trouble on three other fronts—from the Sikhs at Lahore, the Pathans in the Agra area, and from the Mahrattas—encouraged him to hold out.

Consequently, as Bhim Sen procrastinated, negotiations dragged on from May until, at the end of 1815, they collapsed over the issues of yielding the Terai and accepting a British resident in Katmandu. Hastening to explain the delay to London, Moira despatched a 'Secret Letter' to the 'Honourable Secret Committee' of the Honourable East India Company, in which he said: 'The procrastination of the Goorkas [sic] in concluding a treaty is not to be wondered at. The subscribing to the loss of half their Empire is a painful subject for a proud people; so that the prospect of another campaign is now presented to me, by their holding off during a season in which they know we cannot act against them.'

Gurkha success at arms, followed by Gurkha obduracy, had presented the East India Company with a situation unprecedented in its Indian experience. These difficult hillmen must learn to acquiesce and Moira picked Ochterlony to deliver the lesson.

In January 1816 Ochterlony, encouraged by a recent knighthood and a special award of £1,000 a year from the East India Company to enable him to live up to what was at that time a most unusual honour for a Company officer, marched from Dinapore to open a second campaign. His object, to take Katmandu. For all his 20,000 men and 83 guns he faced a testing task. At best only eight weeks remained of the cold-weather campaigning season. Lord Moira had ordered diversionary operations involving 5,000 men in the Terai north of Gorakhpur and a 6,500-strong incursion further west, but Ochterlony's experience told him that two months was an impossibly brief period in which to dislodge such determined defenders from hill fort after hill fort with all the endeavour such campaigning entailed in manhandling and elephant-humping artillery pieces up and down the mountainsides of Nepal. In the circumstances, after passing through the Terai unmolested, he decided to take a daring gamble. Ahead was the heavily defended Bichakori Pass, which any force as large as his would have to take in order to breach the Churia range, beyond which lay Katmandu. However, Ochterlony had heard of an alternative route through the mountains, one which he had been told was familiar to fugitives and hardy smugglers, but which, regarded by Nepal's defenders as too arduous for the passage of an army, had been left unguarded.

Determined to surprise the main Gurkha defences by appearing as if miraculously in their rear and thus open the pass to the mass of his infantry and artillery, Ochterlony set off on the night of 14 February 1816 with two 6-pounder guns on the backs of elephants and 3,000 men. After a night's march ever upwards the force was confronted by a steep 300-foot cliff, which explained to the major-general why only smugglers and fugitives would choose to come

this way. Tempted to return to camp, he reflected again
on the brief campaigning season that remained for settling
this affair with Nepal. Setting a personal example to his
officers and men, the elderly commander began the climb,
clutching his way up from bush to bush, branch by branch.
At the summit, Ochterlony, tentless and without follow-up
food supplies for several days, began to have second
thoughts about the wisdom of his gamble, the ultimate
success of which placed much dependence on the use of
artillery. It seemed impossible that elephants could follow
where the rigours of the ascent had reduced the clothing
and footwear of His Majesty's 87th Foot, the Royal Irish
Fusiliers, to tatters. But Ochterlony had overlooked the
ingenuity of his pioneers who, within two days, not only
dug the steepness out of the hill, but also cut steps into
the less severe incline of their making. Even so the two
artillery elephants, finding they could not keep their
balance on the slope, refused to climb until they had been
unburdened of the 6-pounders on their backs. There was
no alternative but to manhandle the guns up the hillside,
ropes and pulleys being repeatedly repositioned so that the
gun-carriages could be hauled up a few yards at a time.

Fortunately for Ochterlony the Gurkhas, neither hearing
of the ascent nor believing it possible, failed to interrupt
it, and when the defenders of Bichakori Pass discovered
they had been bypassed they fell back on their main force
at Makhwanpur.

Ochterlony's gamble had outwitted Ranjur Singh, his
former opponent at Jaithak, and saved the British column
and most of its elephants from falling into an elaborate
trap which the enemy had set for troops and elephants.
Advancing, the infantry entered a number of stockades
where rock boulders had been stockpiled for rolling down
the hillsides and on to the invaders. Ochterlony's men also
discovered that cool, enticing mountain pools had been
poisoned, but not before several watering elephants had

revealed the trick by their agonised trumpetings.

Gradually the British force, taking Hariharpur on the way, moved up to Makhwanpur where such ferocious fighting took place that it greatly enhanced the steadily increasing mutual respect between the British officers and their Gurkha adversaries.

Individual combat invariably followed a British bayonet charge and Ensign John Shipp of His Majesty's 87th Foot has described his 'hammer and tongs' encounter with a Gurkha leader:

He was a strong and powerful man ... he cut as many capers as a French dancing master. .... At length I made a feint at his toes, to cut them; down went his shield from his face, to save his legs; up went the edge of my sword smack under his chin, in endeavouring to get away from which he threw his head back, which nearly tumbled off, and down he fell. ... I never saw more steadiness or bravery exhibited by any set of men in my life. Run they would not and of death they seemed to have no fear, though their comrades were falling thick around them. ...*

Makhwanpur fell and Bhim Sen sought ratification of the terms which Amar Singh had accepted in the field but which he had overruled from Katmandu.

It was now open to Ochterlony to march on Katmandu and take the Gurkha capital with all the promise of booty that such a prize held, but the British commander, partly through consideration for the health of his troops with the ending of the cold season, passed up the opportunity for enriching himself.

When envoys from Katmandu produced Nepal's copy of the original treaty for ratification Ochterlony exchanged

* *Memoirs of the Extraordinary Military Career of John Shipp* (London, 1894).

it with a copy bearing Lord Moira's signature. Its conditions, while considered harsh by the Gurkhas, were nevertheless face-saving, in that they fell short of demanding British occupation of Katmandu. Thus was preserved the military pride of the Gurkhas, and the foundation laid for the military association between Britain and Nepal which has lasted to this day.

The ten Gurkha rifle regiments, comprising twenty regular and additional wartime battalions which were to soldier for Britain in two world wars, owed their existence to the peace terms which regularised the position of several thousand Gurkhas who, changing sides during the Nepal War, had joined Moira's columns. After the war volunteers were formed into Nasiri, or friendly battalions, chiefly for the purpose of policing the freshly annexed territories of Sirmoor, Garhwal and Kumaon in the western Himalayas; areas which were soon to provide British India with its renowned hill stations of Simla, Mussourie, Almora and Naini Tal.

When India was partitioned in 1947 six of the ten Gurkha regiments remained in the Indian Army and four joined the British Army, with which they still serve.* The circumstances of the origin, in the aftermath of the Nepal War, of one of these regiments, the 2nd King Edward VII's Own Gurkha Rifles, known at first as the Sirmoor Battalion by reason of the neighbourhood in which it was raised, merit especial recall because they reflect the mutual esteem which has since sustained the long and cherished military link between the British Army and its Gurkha comrades.

Shortly after Lieutenant Frederick Young had comforted the dying General Gillespie at Kalunga this officer resumed command of an irregular force which he had raised to assist

*See Appendix 1.

Ochterlony's operations in the west. Young's irregulars, a
hotchpotch of men, sweepings from the available man-
power, were of doubtful military quality and certainly no
match for resolute Gurkhas. Thus, on encountering some
200 Gurkhas, it is no surprise that these irregulars fled
without attempting to engage, leaving Young and his
officers to the mercy of the enemy.

'But why did you not run away too?' the Gurkhas
inquired.

Young replied, 'I have not come so far in order to run
away. I came to stop.'

The British officer then sat down while the Gurkha
commander said thoughtfully, 'We could serve under men
like you.'

Lieutenant Young was taken prisoner and occupied himself learning the language of his captors. After release he
was put in charge of enemy prisoners in the west, and when
his opinion was sought as to what to do with them, he
urged: 'Give me authority first to release the prisoners and
tell them they are free men, and then I will ask them to
volunteer in the Company's service. If they do, and I feel
sure many will, I undertake to raise in a short time a body
of soldiers that will not disgrace you, or the country, or
myself.'

Young then went among the Gurkhas. In his own words,
he 'went there one person and came out 3,000'. Some of
these men formed the Sirmoor Battalion of which Young,
who was to retire as a general, was the first commandant.

'We could serve under men like you.' ... What kind of a
man was this of whom, when news of his death reached
Gurkha regiments almost seventy years afterwards, one
rifleman would say to another, 'Young Sahib was our father
and mother'?

Gazetted in the 2nd Bengal Native Infantry in 1800
Young typified the East India Company's officer class. He
was the son of a clergyman whose great-grandfather, also

a clergyman, had moved from Devon to Northern Ireland in 1660. His daughter recalled: 'Frederick was fortunate in obtaining a cadetship in the East India Company—a rare piece of good fortune in those days, for selections were made with much care. Latin, Greek, mathematics, and foreign languages did not count for much, but a straight shot and good manners went far. The candidates, so far as one could judge from family and surroundings, had to give promise of being men—and particularly gentlemen.'

Before his acceptance as a cadet Young had been interviewed. The interview went like this:

'How old are you?'

'Fifteen on 30th November last.'

'Are you ready to die for king and country?'

'I am.'

'That will do.'

The East India Company had satisfied itself that Frederick Young was a gentleman of whom service in India would make a man, and the Gurkhas were to confirm a faultless selection by recognising their erstwhile captive and future commander—as a sahib.

In time the court of directors of the Honourable East India Company authorised the establishment of Nasiri Gurkha battalions raised at Sabathu near Simla and at Almora in Kumaon. By reason of the districts from which the men were first drawn the recruits, strictly speaking, were not all Gurkhas, many being Garhwalis and Kumaonis. Nevertheless, the Gurkha Brigade of the future owed its origin to the initiative of Frederick Young. Now, as Gurkhas began to enter British service, Moira reminded the Company in London of his deal with the ruler of Oudh. 'This agreement', wrote the Governor-General, 'enables me to assert that the Goorka War [sic] has not cost the company one single shilling.' At the time Moira was not to know just how much of a bargain he had struck. No price can be put on the services Gurkha riflemen were henceforth to render Britain.

CHAPTER TWO

Intrigue at Katmandu

Here, with the conclusion of the Nepal War and the introduction of a Gurkha Brigade in embryo, it is timely to explain how the Gurkhas of the early nineteenth century had come to rule Nepal, especially as their relationship to the tribal system of that country was to influence the pattern of future recruitment.

As the Nepal War opened the Gurkha Empire, centred at Katmandu, was at its peak, stretching from the Sikkim border and the Tista River in the east to the recently conquered western areas from which British India first recruited hillmen, who were not necessarily all Gurkhas. The fighting men who had built this little Himalayan empire, the regular army of Nepal, were of the same stock which thenceforth was to soldier for Britain. The Nepalese Army's officers were Chetris, while its troops were Mongol-featured Magars and Gurungs, hillmen of distinctive tribes in western and central Nepal. However, not all Gurkhas are wholly mongoloid in appearance. This is explained by the admixture of Rajput blood brought about by the arrival of Rajputs in the hills as refugees from the Moslem invasion of India, by the predisposition of Gurkha leaders to seek Rajput wives and by the subsequent recruitment of Rais and Limbus in eastern Nepal. Although mongoloid features predominate, indicating origins north of Tibet, the influence of India is represented in Gurkha food habits and much of Gurkha culture, including music and dances.

It was a Rajput prince, Prithwi Narayan Shah, the Prince of Gorkha, who founded the royal dynasty in the mid-eighteenth century. Although through common usage the name Gurkha has been adopted as the generic term for the soldiers of Nepal, strictly it is a geographical rather than a racial name. In one respect the Gurkha Empire as it was in the early nineteenth century was comparable, however minor in scale, to the Roman Empire. As with the Romans, Gurkha power originated in one town, Gorkha, centrepoint of a small state, but there the analogy ends because Gorkha remained small and insignificant, being wholly over-shadowed by Katmandu, 60 miles to the east in the east-west Nepal valley which was to give its name to the nation. The name Gorkha probably derives from that of Gorakhnath, a saint said to have occupied a cave which Gurkhas regard as a holy place.

Following the Nepal War British India reaped little immediate benefit from its perk of recruiting Gurkhas. This was largely because of political squabbles in Katmandu which precluded the spirited adherence to the letter of the treaty which was to emerge in the Indian Mutiny of 1857 and reach its zenith in the First and Second World Wars. Not until the downfall and death of Bhim Sen Thapa in 1837 was the first article of the treaty to be properly observed. 'There shall be peace and friendship between the Honourable East Indian Company and the Rajah of Nipal,' it read. Yet Bhim Sen's internecine party in-fighting, domination of the ruler and distrust of British intentions, was to postpone development of good relations and a solid alliance until a successor, Jang Bahadur Rana, courted British friendship to the extent of making the long sea journey to England to call on Queen Victoria.

Meanwhile, individual Gurkha fighting men held no inhibitions about campaigning for the East India Company. They wore their new uniforms with pride and, despite Bhim Sen's reluctance to honour the treaty to the letter and lingering British official prejudice against Gurkhas on such diverse grounds as that they were small— never much taller than 5 feet 3 inches—and mercenary, they were given several opportunities to confirm their qualities of courage and loyalty. However, these qualities were not to be accepted beyond all question until after the Indian Mutiny.

Thus Gurkhas, pillbox capped and clad in clove-green jackets with scarlet collars and cuffs, policed the new hill stations and marched in column with East India Company troops against the Mahrattas and Pindaris in 1817-19. It mattered not to the Gurkhas for whom or against whom they fought, providing they were gainfully employed under arms. Some, with the approval of Katmandu, found satisfaction in serving Ranjit Singh, the leader of the Sikhs.

Following the Mahratta war the East India Company's Gurkhas experienced their next major action, at the storming of the great Jat fortress at Bhurtpur in 1826. Twenty years later they surfaced again from routine policing duties to fight the Sikhs. British-employed Gurkhas were so detached from Katmandu and its intrigues with the Sikh state that they fought as though Nepal itself were imperilled, contributing splendidly to victories at Aliwal and Sobraon. Yet, removed though the strong, brave, uncomplicated hillmen were from the domestic power struggle in the Nepal Valley, it was a conflict which merits attention because the outcome was greatly to influence the future of their successors.

The turning-point for improved relations between Nepal and British India came with the suicide in 1837 by kukri of that 'advocate of war', Bhim Sen, who took his life in the Katmandu dungeon where he had been confined at the close of the power struggle. Further disputes there were in the interim, but Bhim Sen's removal made way for change

which would lead eventually to the arrival on the scene of
a soldier's soldier son, Jang Bahadur Rana, who had been
born shortly after the end of the Nepal War.

Jang Bahadur was twenty when Bhim Sen died and
enjoying a wild youth in which gambling and hunting
were his chief pastimes. But then Jang's father lost his
military governorship, which was a setback to Jang's
ambitions. For a while the young officer went absent from
the Nepalese Army to soldier for the Sikhs. Another venture he pursued, aimed at creating an income and paying
off gambling debts, was elephant-catching in the Terai. In
time he returned to Nepal, his arrival coinciding with the
appointment of an uncle, Mahatbar Singh, as prime
minister, and Jang Bahadur became his assistant.

Jang Bahadur now seemed set to succeed his uncle but
there was a problem. Whereas Mahatbar Singh had
received the post by virtue of a queen who was regent for
the mentally defective King Rajendra, their son, the heir
apparent Prince Surendra, hated Jang with an intense
jealousy and was determined to do away with him. Several
unsuccessful murder attempts were followed by an out-
rageous plot to have Jang Bahadur executed by dropping
him into a deep well. Possibly Jang got wind of it, but at
all events he quickly acquired a sporting interest in wells,
jumping into them, wedging himself between the walls, and
practising ascent, descent and plain survival. Thus the
intended victim was not altogether surprised when,
trumping up some charge, Prince Surendra ordered Jang
Bahadur to be put to death by dumping in a well. Believing
such a method of disposal would see the end of his enemy,
the Prince agreed to the condemned man's last request that,
instead of being thrown into the well, he be allowed to
jump down voluntarily. There was a splash and a satisfied
execution party departed. After dark, friends arrived with
a rope. Jang surfaced and went into hiding.

To summarise the conclusion of this period of political

and court intrigue in Katmandu, Jang Bahadur was duly rehabilitated. Then, the mad King Rajendra, imagining that Jang's uncle, the prime minister Mahatbar Singh, was plotting to put Surendra on the throne, ordered Jang to kill his uncle or be put to death himself. The murder plot was set up and Jang, secreted behind a screen in the Queen's home, shot his uncle dead as he arrived to see her. This was in 1845. Jang, knowing that the Queen intended the post for her lover, Gagan Singh, now passed up the opportunity to become prime minister and returned to army service as a general.

King Rajendra's next move was to arrange the murder of the Queen's lover, the outcome of which was a massacre of hundreds of nobles and officials in the Kot, or Royal Court of Assembly, to which they had been summoned by an infuriated queen. The upshot was Jang Bahadur's emergence as prime minister and commander-in-chief and the Queen's subsequent exile together with King Rajendra.

Prince Surendra acceded, but while the prince who had organised Jang's disposal in the well was a mere puppet, Jang Bahadur in 1846 became the master of Nepal. He was only twenty-nine.

Improved relations with Britain formed the basis of Jang Bahadur's foreign policy. Much impressed by the British ability to hold down vast areas of India, the youthful leader of Nepal sought tangible means of demonstrating his admiration of British rule and his desire to be considered as a potentially helpful ally. Thus he was disappointed when in 1848 Lord Dalhousie, the Governor-General, rejected an offer of six regiments to fight alongside British and native regiments in the Second Sikh War. Much frustrated and vexed by this rebuff, Jang Bahadur staged what he termed á 'shooting expedition' in the Terai, but which in effect was an immense manoeuvre involving 30,000 men and 50 guns. The object was to impress the British with the efficiency of his military organisation and to flaunt the force which had been brushed aside.

Jang was now convinced that if he was to promote his ambition of placing Gurkhas at the service of Britain he must make the long journey to London and present himself to Queen Victoria. An official invitation was arranged, and it was a measure of Jang's power and confidence that he felt able to leave Katmandu for almost a year with all the subversion that such an absence might invite. It was also a pointer to his determination to establish a special relationship for his country with Britain that Jang Bahadur was prepared to cross the sea, Hindus then believing that such a journey might lead to bad luck and possibly loss of caste.

Accompanied by two brothers, Dhir Shamsher and Jagat Shamsher, Jang Bahadur sailed for England from Calcutta on 7 April 1850, leaving a brother as acting prime minister and three others in key offices.

The blood on Jang Bahadur Rana's hands was conveniently overlooked as Queen Victoria prepared to welcome him. The fact that he had murdered his uncle on the path to power proved no obstacle to his reception though, as a nicety, he arrived at the Court of St James with the credentials of an ambassador rather than as the totalitarian ruler he had made himself. The visit, which included inspecting a coal-mine and the inevitable seat at the opera, became an incongruous mixture of industrial, agricultural and military education and court circulating, in the course of which Jang so charmed Queen Victoria that she invited him, as if he were a member of the family, to the christening of her third son, Prince Arthur, later Duke of Connaught.

Shortly afterwards the Nepalese leader may possibly have felt even more at home when a deranged subject of Queen Victoria attacked her with a walking-stick. As one who had survived a death sentence by escaping from a well, Jang Bahadur had no qualms about demanding the death penalty for others, and he was surprised when the Queen would not, could not, insist on her guest's request for the immediate execution of her assailant.

Apart from the Queen's constitutional inability to extend such a courtesy, the visit was a great success and sealed, so far as Jang Bahadur and his brother Dhir Shamsher were concerned, by two very special events. While Jang the soldier was to treasure the memory of a conversation with the Duke of Wellington, for his part Dhir Shamsher achieved a personal victory over a wrestling champion whom he had challenged in a London booth.

Katmandu would not have been Katmandu had not a murder plot confronted Jang on his return early in 1851. Sniffing it out with a characteristic nose for such trouble, Jang discovered that, principally, it involved two of his brothers. Possibly he had been influenced by the generally civilising experience of England, and particularly the leniency shown to Queen Victoria's assailant, but his refusal to meet demands for the execution of the con-spirators, and their subsequent exile, astonished the establishment of Katmandu. Mellowed or merely mag-nanimous after his travels abroad, the iron man of Nepal has been recorded as replying to critics of his soft line: 'What would *The Times* say?' It was, however, an obser-vation wholly consistent with Jang Bahadur Rana's desire for personal respect in Britain and his ambition for Gurkhas to do battle henceforth as soldiers of the queen who reigned there.

Problems arising from the 1849 occupation of the Punjab following the Second Sikh War gave the Gurkhas a fresh opportunity to demonstrate how unshakeable was their loyalty to the British paymaster. As anger smouldered in the Bengal native regiments occupying the Punjab because of a reduction of their allowances, and as the 66th Bengal Native Infantry mutinied at Amritsar, Gurkhas moved against the sepoys and enforced the surrender of the rebels.

In reward the Gurkhas received the greatest possible honour—possession of the 66th's colours and title and with them the privilege of parading in the scarlet coats of that regiment.

Before very long Gurkhas, not only of the battalions raised in Sirmoor and Kumaon, but also belonging to regiments sent to the East India Company's assistance in India by allied Nepal, were to play a courageous, often decisive role in putting down the mutiny of mutinies which was so radically to change the system of British rule in India.

CHAPTER THREE

The Indian Mutiny, 1857

By the time the Bengal native units of the garrison at Meerut mutinied on 11 May 1857 Gurkhas of the Sirmoor and Kumaon Battalions and the 66th Gurkha Regiment of the Bengal Army had already set themselves apart spiritually and, where possible, physically from the East India Company's native troops. Shortly before the Indian Mutiny, Gurkhas improving their musketry on a course at Ambala, had emphasised their desire to be regarded as the equals of European soldiers by successfully asking permission to pitch their tents together with those of British troops. Although generally conscious of their superiority to Bengal native infantry, or black folk as they disparagingly labelled them, on this occasion the Gurkha riflemen were influenced by a special consideration.

There was much unrest among the native sepoys about the use of greased cartridges issued as ammunition for the new Enfield rifle and the Gurkhas, wishing to have no part in such agitation, after being allowed to sleep in the British lines, further demonstrated their disdain for the sepoys by demanding greased cartridges even though offered ungreased ones as substitutes. Thus, as discontent within the Bengal Army over the issue of greased cartridges reached its peak, Gurkhas had already made it clear where their loyalty lay. Although Hindu by religion, paramountly they

were professional soldiers and, as such, were not prepared
to allow themselves to be suborned by political agitators
who were playing on religious taboos of Hindus and
Moslems alike. For what had happened was that political
opponents of the East India Company, with its spreading
grasp of the subcontinent, had seized on the loading
requirement of riflemen to bite the cap from each greased
cartridge as an instrument for destroying British rule. Sub-
versively, they had sown the seeds of revolt by suggesting
that, in biting the cap, riflemen were tasting grease
manufactured from the fat of pigs and cows.

After razing Meerut, more than 20,000 mutineers swept
down on Delhi, 40 miles to the south, to find that a
separate uprising had deprived them of a second opportunity to massacre European families. As they arrived
Delhi was already in the hands of mutineers and only time,
and with its passage the arrival, among other reinforcements, of Gurkhas marching from the depot at Dehra Dun,
would relieve it.

The Sirmoor Battalion, accompanied by two elephants
humping ammunition extra to the sixty rounds each rifleman carried in his pouches, marched on Meerut from the
foothills of the Himalayas within four hours of news of the
Mutiny reaching its commandant, Major Charles Reid.

The column travelled light, Reid's sense of urgency
ruling out tents and other impedimenta. It was as well
because Major Reid, hearing that Brigadier-General Sir
Archdale Wilson's brigade making for Delhi from Meerut
was at risk to superior numbers of mutineers, was obliged
to hasten to the rescue along a route which had been flooded
by saboteurs of the irrigation system. Into the murky waters
plunged the little Gurkhas, stumbling, gurgling, often near
drowning, their rifles held above their heads. Eventually,
7 miles miles outside Delhi, they glimpsed the scarlet
facings on the uniforms of the British 60th Rifles belonging
to Wilson's brigade.

The Mutiny was not confined to Delhi and its immediate district. From mid-May until early June native regiments revolted from the Punjab to the middle Ganges, in which area Cawnpore and Lucknow were besieged by dissident troops. At the end of June Cawnpore surrendered under promise of safe conduct out of the city, but European men were treacherously massacred and women and children taken prisoner. Thus, by July 1857, action resulting from the Mutiny was centred on two sieges—that of Delhi by inferior numbers of British and loyal native troops, and that of Lucknow by mutineers.

Given but a few hours respite after their long march, Major Reid's Gurkhas linked up with the 60th Rifles and drove the rebels back to the city walls. Then they occupied a position overlooking the city, known as the Ridge. Here the Gurkhas established a stronghold at a deserted home known as Hindu Rao's House, formerly the home of a nobleman.

Sustained efforts were made to dislodge the Gurkhas from their position on the Ridge, and when at last the mutineers began to despair of defeating them they cried out, 'Come and join us. We won't fire on you'. The Gurkhas shouted 'We are coming' and the mutineers, believing they had won them over, awaited the arrival of such welcome defectors. However, when they were but the length of a cricket-pitch away, the Gurkhas deluged the rebel native troops with rifle-fire and chased them back into Delhi in a ferocious kukri charge.

Day after day in temperatures reaching 131°F at noon Reid and his Gurkhas, reinforced at times by companies of the 60th Rifles, Coke's Rifles and the Guides, repelled further determined attacks on their Ridge position. Thousands, as Reid recorded, 'against a mere handful of men'.

Before the Gurkhas had proved themselves at Delhi, senior British officers, not accustomed to serving with the hillmen from Nepal and disillusioned by the disloyalty of the Indian native regiments, had been sufficiently distrustful as to encamp them under the guns of the artillery. But now to these same officers Gurkhas became 'splendid little fellows' and every kukri charge they made was cheered to the echo by their British comrades.

By June, sixteen days after the onset of repeated sallies against Hindu Rao's House, the Gurkhas, warming to the enthusiastic reception of their valour, were ever ready to exceed the previous day's exploits. Never again would any British commander entertain doubts about their loyalty or fighting quality. God send us more Gurkhas was the prayer of the hour, and shortly it was to be answered. On 23 June the Kumaon Battalion was ordered from Rawalpindi to Delhi. And from Katmandu two Nepalese regiments marched into India to fight for Queen Victoria as and when required.

If a certain public cynicism attends the exchange of state visits nowadays, such courtesies were not without their value in the last century. The men of the Sirmoor and Kumaon Battalions were already under British arms and receiving British pay as they fought alongside British troops during the Mutiny, but the Nepalese Army belonged to an independent state which, far from having any direct interest in continued British rule in India, might, while its old soldiers remembered the invasion of their country, have been gratified by its demise. However, Jang Bahadur's London visit had so improved Nepal's relations with imperial Britain that, as news of the Mutiny reached the Nepalese prime minister he recognised in it the supreme test of Gurkha loyalty to his friend Queen Victoria. He also welcomed an opportunity for providing gainful employment for a reserve of trained Gurkhas restive for action and reward.

In June, as the battle raged for possession of the Ridge, General Dhir Shamsher, hero of the wrestling challenge in a London booth, marched with 3,000 men on Gorakhpur, disarmed the mutineers and occupied the rebel-held areas at Jaunpur and Azamgarh. Later, as will be seen, his brother, Jang Bahadur, was to place himself at the head of some 10,000 men and to play a decisive part in relieving Lucknow. Immediately, though, reinforcement was imperative at Delhi. Here, in June, July, August and most of September, the Gurkhas were to throw back 26 major attacks by the mutineers for the loss of 8 out of 9 officers and 327 out of 490 men in killed or wounded. By 29 June, when the Gurkha wounded were evacuated, Reid's battalion had been reduced to 200 men. Even the most experienced soldiers suffered grievous injuries, among them Subedar-Major Singhbir Thapa who so many years ago had fought against Moira's army at Kalunga. It was with intense relief that the Sirmoor survivors welcomed men freshly recruited for their own unit—and the Kumaon Battalion.

At 3 am on the first day of August the Kumaon Battalion, some 500-strong, splashed through the monsoon puddles and on to the Ridge. After a punishing march in heat and through the rains the Gurkhas had covered 500 miles in just over five weeks as escort to a column of artillery, ammunition and treasure from Rawalpindi. But there was to be no rest. Within hours of their arrival outside Delhi the battalion was in action.

Religious considerations had inspired the Delhi mutineers throughout and this day their fanaticism was given a further fillip by the celebration of the Moslem festival of Id. Appreciating that under such stimulus he could expect great things of the men, the aged King of Delhi—formerly a British puppet and now reasserting himself on the backs

of the mutineers—encouraged a massive assault on the
Ridge. From their look-out at Hindu Rao's House the
Gurkhas gave the alarm that something unusual was
happening; that artillery accompanied by up to 10,000
troops was coming out of the city.

When the attack came it did not abate for twenty-four
hours. Incident followed incident with such rapidity that
Major Reid, passing a telescope to an orderly so that he
could reach for a cup of tea, had no time to be distressed
by his sudden discovery that the orderly's head had been
shot off and the tea-bearer's chest ripped through by a
bullet. It was during the Id offensive, too, that Reid found
a wounded fourteen-year-old Gurkha boy holding an exposed outpost. Curious as to how such a boy came to be
not merely in the battle but at the very forefront of it, Reid
discovered that he had loaded for his father until his father
had been killed. Then he had loaded for a rifleman of the
60th until the British soldier had been too severely
wounded to fight on. Thereafter the Gurkha boy had
taken over the rifle until he was himself wounded. The
boy was a 'line boy'—that is, one who had been born in the
Sirmoor Battalion lines at Dehra Dun and had marched
to India with his father. Major Reid enlisted him on the
spot, one of many such line boys who would take with
pride the place of their fathers.

In August and September further reinforcements and a
train of siege artillery arrived, and at their head was
Brigadier-General John Nicholson, the Lion of the Punjab,
who had earned the great respect of the Sikhs because of
his exploits against them in the Second Sikh War. Nicholson, aged only thirty-four, was supposedly subordinate to
Archdale Wilson, but such was his forceful personality that
he urged and planned the storming of Delhi, an operation
which he had decided must feature Gurkhas. From his
arrival Nicholson had been much impressed by their
military style and Reid's account of their record. He had

also noted with satisfaction an intelligence report that the King of Delhi had put a price of 10 rupees on every Gurkha head, a going rate which equated fighting qualities of the hillmen from Nepal with those of their British comrades.

At the age of eighty-two the King, who as if at some panoramic tattoo at times followed the progress of the battle from a grandstand position, had made a fair assessment of the market. From the opening of the bombardment of his strongpoints on 11 September until clearing-up parties had stopped all resistance nine days later, Gurkhas and their good friends of the 60th Rifles were at the sharp end of the offensive. Major Reid, though wounded, was carried to safety on the back of one of his men. Brigadier-General Nicholson, who had insisted on a spearhead role for the Gurkhas, died with them. Leading an assault force, the Lion of the Punjab was killed brandishing his sword on the very ramparts of Delhi.

From Delhi, Gorakhpur, indeed from wherever Gurkhas of the Indian and Nepalese Armies were engaged, reports of such individual steadfastness and general military ability filtered through to Lord Canning, the Governor-General who exercised overall responsibility for suppressing the Mutiny from Government House in Calcutta. The reports were so frequent and so universal in their praise of Gurkhas that, in December 1857, Canning felt confident enough to entrust Jang Bahadur and his 14 infantry battalions and 4 artillery batteries, totalling 24 guns, with operations in the much disaffected province of Oudh and, subsequently, with a leading role in securing the relief of Lucknow.

By the middle of March 1858 Jang Bahadur's campaigning had been so successful that there remained little for his army to do, and Canning was faced with providing suitable rewards for the Nepalese prime minister's services. In the event, Jang Bahadur had to wait two years for official recognition, which came in the form of a knighthood, a distinction much coveted by friendly orientals—and also for the return to Nepal of the 200-mile strip of the Terai which had been part of Bhim Sen's surrender package after the Nepal War. More immediately Canning acquiesced to the removal from India of large quantities of loot and the provision of British troops to escort the heavily laden Gurkhas, together with several thousand bullock-carts, across their borders. The irreverent, rough British soldiery swore that the great bullock-train contained caskets of jewels looted by Jang Bahadur from the prostitutes' quarter of Lucknow. Whatever the validity of such allegations, it is known that henceforth the ruling Rana possessed a magnificent collection of jewellery.

CHAPTER FOUR

Serving the Queen Empress

When the British troops had seen their Gurkha friends safely home, and the Mutiny was over, the army in India had to shake itself out and begin to conform with customs and regulations consequent upon the ending of East India Company rule. In 1858 Her Majesty's Government took over executive responsibility for Indian affairs and Queen Victoria, who was not to be proclaimed empress until 1877, became Queen of India.

The change-over brought the beginnings of the Gurkha Brigade which was to fight in two world wars, and which was to be kept in force to this day—though in a much depleted state. Since the time of the Nepal War recruitment of Gurkhas for British service had been as haphazard and opportunist as Frederick Young's selection of Gurkha prisoners and Major Reid's field enlistment under fire of a line boy. But now that the Indian Army served the Crown, uniformity was required and its needs were, in time, to change cherished privileges and traditions. For instance, whereas the Sirmoor Battalion, the 2nd Gurkhas, was styled a rifle regiment after the Mutiny, the Malaun Battalion, the 1st Gurkhas, was not obliged to give up its much-prized scarlet coats—inherited, it will be recalled, from the disaffected 66th Bengal Native Infantry—until 1888. Nor were all Gurkha regiments officially designated

rifle regiments until 1891. Meanwhile, years of campaigning lay ahead, in which example would found fresh
traditions and provide a firm basis for the legends attending
the Gurkha Brigade.

Immediately, the North-West Frontier of India offered
a natural and convenient exercise area for Gurkha qualities.
The hardy hillmen made ideal adversaries for Afghan and
Pathan warriors who were displaying an almost sporting
delight in harassing the trade routes which linked British
India, Afghanistan and parts of Asia. As had been learned
during the Mutiny, Gurkhas preferred to align themselves
with European troops. Holding natives other than themselves in great disdain they were prepared to do battle with
any enemy of Queen Victoria.

In addition to the first three regiments of Gurkhas a
fourth had been raised in the emergency of the Mutiny and
now, as the Indian Army settled down to the frontier warfare phase of its existence, the Gurkha Brigade began to
grow and take shape: at first by the expediency of gathering
individual Gurkhas from other units into exclusively
Gurkha battalions and later by direct recruitment. Thus
the Hazara Gurkha Battalion, later the 5th Gurkhas, which
emerged from the bringing together of former irregulars,
took its place in the Punjab Frontier Force, and demonstrated the frontier value of Gurkhas in the Mahsud Waziri
campaign of 1860. Equally, such campaigning served to
build Gurkha confidence in the young officers sent out from
Britain to lead them.

Gurkhas who fought the Mahsud Waziris were to pass
on from father to son the story of Captain Charles Keyes,
who engaged the Waziri leader in single combat as the
battle was going badly for his men. Mesmerised by the
sword duel the Gurkhas and other Indian Army troops
stopped fighting and watched until the Waziri fell and his
7,000 followers, taking to their heels, sought refuge in the
mountains.

Most campaigns of this period managed to produce heroic encounters of the genre which inspired Victorian and Edwardian writers of adventure stories. Yet isolated moments of derring-do, such as Keyes's destruction of his Waziri opponent, were interspersed by months and years of hardship in an appalling climate and of long marches over difficult terrain. Such demands were typified by the experience of the former Kumaon Battalion, the 3rd Gurkhas, towards the end of 1864 when the Tibetan-border state of Bhutan became a candidate for punishment for countenancing repeated raids on British territory. Obstinate resistance prolonged the presence of a British force in Bhutan's pestilential swamps and heavily wooded hills, the climate accounting for a heavy sick-list before Bhutan promised to behave and peace was made.

The punitive expeditions of the 1860s and 1870s served the dual purposes of founding field traditions of hardiness for the Gurkha Brigade and consolidating the communities which were developing around the recently created regimental centres of the 1st Gurkhas at Dharmsala, the 2nd at Dehra Dun, the 3rd at Almora and the 4th at Bakloh. Gurkha, and in the time British families, were to grow up alongside one another in the Eden of the Himalayan foothills, their men returning from the ravages of frontier duties to the delights of hill-station life.

Throughout this period Jang Bahadur Rana continued whole-heartedly to encourage British recruitment of Gurkhas and early in 1875 would have embarked on a second visit to Queen Victoria had he not suffered a serious chest injury in a riding accident at Bombay. However, a year afterwards Queen Victoria consoled Jang by sending the Prince of Wales to visit him. Jang marked the honour with a great tiger shoot in the Terai, the Prince's enjoyment so enhancing the already very warm relations between Britain and Nepal that when Queen Victoria was proclaimed Empress of India on 1 January 1877 Gurkha riflemen were much in evidence at the Delhi ceremonies.

Sadly, the festivities were hardly finished when Jang Bahadur Rana developed a fever and died. As the funeral pyre blazed on the banks of the holy Baghmati stream the great Gurkha leader's three senior wives threw themselves into the flames, committing sati, a practice which had been forbidden by law in British India since 1829. The farewell words of the most senior wife have been handed down: 'Gentlemen, you all know the love the Maharajah had for you, and the zeal with which he devoted his life to the welfare of your country. If in the discharge of his duty he has ever by word, look or deed wronged any one of you, I, on his behalf, ask you to forgive him and join me in praying for the everlasting peace of his soul.'

Jang Bahadur had personified the martial virtues which British officers were henceforth to extol in Gurkhas under their command, and none with greater admiration than Major-General Sir Frederick Roberts, who as a twenty-four-year-old lieutenant of artillery, had commended the Gurkhas' bravery at Delhi and whose Victoria Cross in the Mutiny had attracted their reciprocal esteem. Thus, when on 21 November 1878 Britain made war on Afghanistan following the armed rejection of her military mission in favour of a Russian counterpart at Kabul, Roberts regarded a Gurkha element as indispensable to the three columns which comprised the punitive expedition.

The plan, as the history books would simplify it, was for the three British columns to march on Kabul through the Khyber and Peiwar Passes and on Kandahar from the area of Quetta, but the hardships of such an undertaking, which can never be written into orders, would long precede the appearance of the Afghan enemy, as the experience of the 3rd Gurkhas exemplifies.

Ordered from Almora on 12 October 1878 the regiment, after a tedious road, rail and steamer journey, reached the northern banks of the Indus south of Quetta on 26

November. Yet even then it seemed to the men that they were only at the outset of their travels, because they were now faced with a 200-mile march across the Dera Bugti desert accompanied by a supply column of hundreds of camels. Then, having arrived in the area of Quetta, the main march, which would carry them through the Bolan Pass and over the Khoja Amran range to Kandahar, lay ahead. This was to prove so testing that bullocks heaving the 40-pounder guns, their hooves bleeding from the terrain, broke down and had to be replaced by Gurkhas. Indeed, the privations of the column were so severe that its subsequent sufferings from snow and short rations as it probed beyond Kandahar were accepted as the lesser evils. Considering the conditions it was possibly as well that in this phase of the war the Kandahar column encountered scant opposition—in contrast with Major-General Roberts's column moving up the Kurram Valley.

Highlanders from two ends of the earth, the Gurkhas of Nepal and the Seaforths from Scotland, shared the honours in the storming of a pair of precipitous escarpments which were the principal features of Roberts's advance. The first engagement resulted from a turning movement led by Roberts himself against a strongly fortified Afghan position known as the Spingawai Kotal. In freezing conditions and a biting wind the Gurkhas and Seaforths stumbled up through icy streams and ever upwards through the night until there, above them on a hillside, stood the enemy. As the Afghans opened fire the Gurkhas drew their kukris and, overtaking the breathless Scots, charged up the hill, taking their direction from the flashes of enemy gunfire. At sunrise the position belonged to Roberts.

Roberts's next objective was the Peiwar Kotal, an even more difficult escarpment which the Afghans had fortified as their main defensive position on this route to Kabul. Again Roberts resorted to the tactic of a turning movement, helped on this occasion by mountain artillery. If decorations for gallantry in Gurkha regiments were not as routine as they were to become, they were already frequent, and for these actions the 5th Gurkhas collected a Victoria Cross for Captain John Cook and an Indian Order of Merit—the Indian soldier's Victoria Cross—for each of five Gurkhas.

Shortly afterwards it was learned that the suspect Russian mission had departed from Kabul and that Sher Ali, the Afghan ruler who had courted Russian friendship, had died. A British mission was accepted by Sher Ali's son and successor, Yakub Khan, who, appearing to be more amenable, received a guarantee of British protection against Russia under a treaty signed on 26 May 1879.

With the exception of the 3rd Gurkhas who were three days out from Kandahar on the return march to India, British forces had been withdrawn from Afghanistan when in September 1879 Sir Louis Cavagnari, the British envoy to Kabul, and his escort of Guides cavalry and infantry, died defending themselves against disaffected Afghan troops intent upon looting the British residency.

Inevitably hostilities were resumed and as inevitably Gurkhas and Scottish Highlanders, the Seaforths and the Gordons, were largely responsible for defeating the enemy in key actions which achieved the occupation of Kabul and the relief of a British force besieged in Kandahar. While the 5th Gurkhas were involved in the Battle of Charasia, where the defeat by some 4,000 men of the main Afghan army 100,000-strong opened the road to Kabul for Roberts, the 3rd Gurkhas, marching from Kandahar to Kabul, averted disaster for their column by withstanding a fanatical cavalry and infantry attack in which the Afghans used the advantage of the heights above the route.

There, on 19 April 1880, in a remote and rocky wilderness, as the entire British force was in peril of being hacked to pieces, the voice of Colonel H. H. Lyster, VC, of the 3rd Gurkhas, rang out: 'Form company squares, fours deep, on the centre close, double march.' Absent from Almora for almost two years they remembered their drill and responded with the precision and discipline of the parade-ground. After a bloody battle the Afghans withdrew.

Just as it seemed that the Afghan problem had been resolved, news reached Kabul that Yakub Khan's brother Ayub, marching on Kandahar, had defeated a small British force at Maiwand and laid siege to the city. The onus was on Roberts to clear up the mess and when, in the heat of August, he set out on his celebrated Kabul-to-Kandahar march of 303 miles in twenty days, the 2nd, 4th and 5th Gurkhas were in the relief force.

At Kandahar it was a rifleman of the 2nd Gurkhas who rounded off the greatly enhanced reputation which the Afghan fighting had brought to the brave little men. Charging the line of Afghan guns alongside comrades of the Gordon Highlanders, a soldier of the 2nd Gurkhas, determined to demonstrate that his regiment had got there first, shoved his cap down an Afghan muzzle and shouted, 'This gun belongs to the 2nd Gurkhas—Prince of Wales!'

At the close of the campaign Sir Frederick Roberts—he was knighted after Peiwar Kotal and became a baronet after Kandahar—had a special word for the Gurkhas and the Scots in his farewell address to the force. He said: 'You beat them at Kabul, and you have beaten them at Kandahar, and now as you are about to leave the country, you may be assured that the very last troops the Afghans ever want to meet in the field are Scottish Highlanders and Gurkhas'. Twelve years afterwards, in 1892, when he was created Baron Roberts of Kandahar—Lord Roberts received an earldom in 1900 after the Boer War—'Bobs', as he was affectionately known throughout the empire, selected a Gurkha and a Gordon Highlander as the left- and right-hand supporters of his coat of arms. It was a soldier's acknowledgement of his debt to his favourite Highlanders.

When Roberts cited the dread in which Afghan soldiers held their Gurkha adversaries he had already determined to advocate greatly increased recruitment from Nepal. He was convinced that there was no enemy of the Queen Empress who would not wilt before a kukri charge, and in 1885 his appointment as Commander-in-Chief, India, gave him the opportunity to launch his cherished Gurkha expansion scheme. Resumed fears of Russian designs on Afghanistan imparted a special urgency to building a brigade of such good soldiers and the Indian Army was authorised to raise second battalions of each of the five regiments. Although the Prime Minister, Maharaja Bhir Shamsher, son of Jang's youngest brother Dhir Shamsher, maintained his family's policy of offering the Nepalese Army's services whenever and wherever a threat to British India appeared, Roberts insisted on picking and choosing his own recruits and subjecting them to British training and discipline. If the Nepalese leader was piqued he did not remain so for long. A present of cash and a delivery of rifles and ammunition for the Nepalese Army quickly restored his goodwill.

In the event the Russian threat failed to amount to more than sporadic border incursions and the incitement of tribes to irritate British border patrols, but it had the useful effect of stimulating a recruitment system which would be capable of swift development in a crisis.

As depots were established at Ghoom near Darjeeling and at Gorakhpur, young Gurkhas volunteered in their hundreds and some of them would be Viceroy's Commissioned Officers and highly trained members of their regiments when they sailed to Europe and took their place in the front line of the war which Britain declared on Germany on 4 August 1914. Meanwhile there would follow campaigns, from the experience of which Gurkhas and their British officers could stock up the regimental and brigade *esprit de corps* which, as they faced unaccustomed conditions and weapons during the First World War, was at times just about all they would have to sustain them.

For the 4th Gurkhas there was no respite after the relief of Kandahar, because they were involved immediately in subduing restless tribesmen in Baluchistan, but for the 1st, 2nd and 3rd Gurkhas there was a period of recruitment and camps of exercise—a form of intensive training much favoured by Roberts—until unfriendly actions on the part of King Thebaw of Burma necessitated a march on Mandalay.

When the 3rd Gurkhas were ordered to Burma the regiment had recently completed the return march from Almora to Meerut for a camp of exercise conducted by the Duke of Connaught, Queen Victoria's third son, whose christening, it will be recalled, Jang Bahadur had attended in London.

King Thebaw's chief crimes were that he had intrigued with the French, acted unjustly towards British traders and fined the British-owned Bombay and Burma Trading Company, imprisoning some of its British staff. The occupation of Mandalay, seizure and deportation of King Thebaw and annexation by the Crown of Upper Burma was swiftly achieved, but counter-guerilla operations dragged on, occupying the 3rd Gurkhas and Gurkha reinforcements from a Bengal Native Infantry regiment, later the 8th Gurkhas, in Burma for a year.

With the Burma affront to British interests settled, Gurkhas of the Indian Army were very soon embroiled again in frontier disputes. These arose frequently because the British presence inevitably angered tribesmen who had for so long held sway in the remote and lawless regions along the North-West and North-East Frontiers of India.

Experience in Afghanistan had shown to what great advantage the short strong legs of the stocky hillmen from Nepal could be put in mountainous country where a main force and its artillery were restricted to routes and passes vulnerable to ambush from above. As a party or column picked its way through scrub and boulders, Gurkhas scouted ahead, ascending and descending with an ease lacking in most other troops, although the Gurkhas much admired the nimbleness of comrades of the Scottish Highland regiments in this respect.

There was something else that Gurkhas had cause to appreciate in the 'wee jocks' from Scotland and the traditions they had brought to the North-West Frontier. This was the stirring, sometimes haunting music of their pipe bands, and they adopted the bagpipe and its accompanying drums. In 1888 the 3rd Gurkhas were granted permission to form a pipe band on the strict understanding that the pipers were on no account to lose their efficiency as fighting soldiers. Prospective Gurkha pipers were sent on a six-month course with a Highland corps, and by November 1889 the band of the 3rd Gurkhas had achieved sufficient competence to give 200 riflemen drawn from the regiment's two battalions a rousing send-off as they marched to the roof of the world to investigate supposed frontier infringements by Tibet. The expedition was an armed reconnaissance to confirm reports that Tibet had fortified a position on the British side of the border at Niti. After three weeks of marching at heights of up to 18,000 feet, possibly the greatest altitude ever reached by a body of disciplined troops, the Gurkhas found that the outpost was no more than a wind-break to protect a trade route camping-ground from the atrocious weather. The riflemen were disappointed that there had been no fighting, but the march had served to demonstrate that there appeared to be no limits to the endurance of British-trained Gurkhas.

CHAPTER FIVE

Frontier Campaigns, 1897–1904

Within a year a rather more serious situation at Imphal along the borders of India and Burma offered Gurkhas an opportunity to display somewhat different qualities to those which had brought them recognition as experts in North-West Frontier operations. Imphal was the capital of the small independent state of Manipur, lying between Burma and Assam, and it was from here that the Raja, losing power to his chief minister known as the Senapati, fled and requested aid. Assistance was given in the form of 400 Gurkhas of Bengal Native Infantry units which were later to become the 6th and 8th Gurkhas. Their orders were to march on Imphal, join up with 60 Gurkhas who were already there as protectors of the British residency, and to arrest the Senapati. Thirty more residency Gurkhas were stationed just outside Imphal.

However, the arrest did not take place. Invited for talks by the Senapati, following an exchange of fire between Gurkhas and a Manipuri garrison, a British party of seven arresting officers, among them the Chief Commissioner for Assam, were seized and beheaded. In the confusion that followed, two British officers who had remained with the troops marched about 150 Gurkhas away, inexplicably leaving some 300 leaderless riflemen to face 5,000 Manipuris. There followed an action which confirmed that, even

57

though they might be deprived of their British officers, Gurkhas were ready to stand and fight to the death against impossible odds. The Gurkhas maintained steady rifle-fire against the Manipuris so long as their ammunition lasted, and then they drew their kukris and fought hand-to-hand until, by sheer weight of numbers, the 50 Gurkhas still left on their feet were overwhelmed.

When they realised what had happened, members of the Gurkha party outside Imphal, which also had no British officer, acted with great initiative. Led by Jemadar Birbal Nagarkoti, the 30 men fought their way out of a Manipuri trap and marched to bring news of the disaster to the nearest Indian Army detachment, 50 Madras infantrymen led by a Lieutenant Grant. Courageously this combined force of 85 men, 3 supply elephants and Lieutenant Grant defied the Manipuris for eleven days until joined by a relief force which included 100 riflemen of the 2/4th Gurkhas. Imphal was re-entered, the Senapati was executed, Grant received the Victoria Cross, and Jemadar Birbal the Order of British India. Of greater significance, it was noted that Gurkhas could not only act on any going but do so on their own initiative.

The Commander-in-Chief, India, was well pleased. Gurkhas had more than justified his decision to expand recruitment and add a second battalion to each regiment. Their every action was attended by good reports as Roberts, remembering Gurkha exploits at Delhi during the Mutiny, had known it would be. Now, thirty-five years on, Lord Roberts was preparing to resign as commander-in-chief and say good-bye to India. The Government wished him to remain, but Roberts had spent only eighteen months out of India in a quarter of a century and, since regulations forbade leave for a C-in-C, only resignation would get him back to England. However, there remained one final and important function for him to fulfil, and this was to foster the goodwill of Nepal that had been already nourished. In effect this meant establishing a personal relationship with the ruling Rana prime minister and his family in Katmandu, because upon their co-operation depended the continuing presence of the best native troops in British service. Fortunately, Roberts had received what he described as 'the very unusual honour of an invitation to Katmandu' from the Prime Minister, Maharaja Bhir Shamsher.

In these times Katmandu, careful to protect Nepal's isolation, and since the Nepal War always retaining an inner reserve about possible British intentions, made no effort to improve the route from Nepal's borders with British India to the capital. Consequently, before reaching the valley, Lord and Lady Roberts were obliged to make the last stages of their 100-mile journey from the border post of Segauli very much as if they were Gurkha soldiers returning on leave, dropping in some places, as Roberts noted, from rock to rock.

For all the outward graciousness that Lord and Lady Roberts encountered in Katmandu—'the manners of well-bred gentlemen', the operas, the plaintive Nepalese airs—the rugged nature of the road to the capital was well matched by the ruthlessness at the political top. The Prime Minister and his family were as ready to shed blood to gain or retain their positions as was any kukri-wielding Gurkha to decapitate an enemy of the Queen Empress. Indeed, while it was of no concern to Roberts or to the Gurkhas he wanted for his army, murder had placed Bhir Shamsher in power. As already mentioned, Bhir Shamsher was the son of the great Jang Bahadur's youngest brother, Dhir Shamsher, and had succeeded yet another of Jang's brothers, Rana Udip Singh, after Udip had been murdered for the purpose of empowering the Shamsher branch of the family. Thereafter Roberts's host had put a number of his opponents to death. As Roberts noted, the King of Nepal continued to be of no executive account, the ruling Ranas having conveniently converted the throne into an object of holy veneration, the king 'a handsome lad of about 18 years of age', Roberts observed, being dressed not in uniform but in a plain dress of spotless white and 'being considered too sacred to be troubled with mundane affairs'. But the Prime Minister and his brother, General Chandra Shamsher, were only too willing to discuss military matters, Bhir Shamsher impressing upon Lord Roberts that the Nepalese Army was at the disposal of the Queen Empress and the general astonishing Lady Roberts with the bald question 'When are the Russians coming? I wish they would make haste. We have 40,000 soldiers in Nepal ready for war and there is no one to fight'. If Russian failure to test the Gurkhas and the Nepalese Army had disappointed Chandra Shamsher, 'a very red hot soldier' as Roberts described him, he never relaxed his efforts to provide an outlet for their military talents and desires, and was delighted when in 1914 the German Kaiser supplied it.

On his return to England Roberts was promoted to field-marshal, and, following further distinction in the Boer War, was rewarded with an earldom and the Garter. He was ever reminded of the Gurkhas by the gold-mounted kukri presented to him in Nepal, and carried his admiration of 'our best class of native soldiers' to the War Office and to Queen Victoria herself.

Cumulative frontier troubles followed Roberts's visit to Nepal and kept Gurkha regiments busily employed together with British and Indian Army regiments. Britain was touchy about any possibility of loss of ground or face in the remote rocky wastes of the North-West Frontier regions, in which the British, Russian and Chinese Empires chafed each other. Much expense, effort and enterprise were devoted to charging, shelling and lecturing recalcitrant tribesmen that, where British troops and British-officered native troops marched and manned garrisons, British rule of law must be respected. Thus, in 1895,

Gurkhas of the 2/2nd, 1/4th and 2/4th helped to force the heavily defended Malakand Pass and relieve a fort in Chitral which had been invested by Kohistan tribesmen.

Two years afterwards there was widespread trouble along hundreds of miles of the North-West Frontier when Moslem tribesmen, partly inspired by Turkey's defeat of Greece, launched a fanatical offensive. Their attacks were particularly difficult to counter because the tribesmen believed that they were impervious to British bullets; that only Islam doubters would die. It took 70,000 troops, among whom were battalions from five Gurkha regiments, two years to restore peace to a region where tribesmen had regarded trade caravans as fair game until British escorts and garrisons were introduced. 'The relationship between troops and tribes', as Philip Mason has described it, 'was one of punishers and punished. . . . The little wars of the Frontier which arose from this system were the staple fare of the Indian Army for the Victorian period.'*

One such war was the campaign of 1897–8 against the Afridis in Tirah, tribesmen who, reneging on an agreement to help the Government of India keep open the Khyber Pass into Afghanistan, had sacked forts in that area. Among the considerable problems attending such an expedition was a lack of knowledge about the wild mountainous region carved with treacherous defiles and in defence of which resistance could be expected from up to 50,000 tribesmen. In these conditions success would depend on efficient scouting, the only reconnaissance available before the advent of aerial methods, and this is where the Gurkhas showed that they could excel.

The Gurkhas were represented in General Sir William Lockhart's Tirah force of some 40,000 British and native troops by one battalion apiece from the first five regiments and also by the 9th Regiment. From these regiments 120 men of the 3rd and 5th Gurkhas were picked to form the

* *A Matter of Honour* (Jonathan Cape, 1974).

body of Gurkha Scouts. This elite unit was expanded until it was 500 strong. It was the first time the army in India had organised a specialised body of scouts.

Towards the close of the nineteenth century Gurkha qualities were still little known in Britain and Colonel H. D. Hutchinson, formerly commanding the 2/3rd Gurkhas, felt it necessary to explain the role of the Gurkha Scouts in his book on the campaign.* They were, he wrote, 'specially trained to work on the steepest hillsides and selected for their wiry physique, fleetness of foot, and skill as marksmen. Their careful preparation in peacetime had made them hardy, active, intelligent, self-reliant, and resolute, and throughout the expedition, under the bold leadership of their officers, they were conspicuous by their dash and daring, both in attack and defence'.

An especial hazard of the Tirah capaign was the sharpness of Afridi tribesmen in picking off unsuspecting troops as they camped. To counter this disturbing practice, Gurkhas in plain clothes stalked the snipers with rifle and kukri.

Each frontier campaign could be reckoned to produce an heroic episode of a character which appealed strongly to Victorian armchair followers of daring deeds. Typical incidents were recorded in books such as Hutchinson's, and in the following example, taken from Hutchinson's earlier despatches to *The Times*. In Tirah, the storming of the Dargai heights by the 1/2nd Gurkhas and the 1st Gordon Highlanders contained the classic ingredients of popular frontier non-fiction.

The Afridis had fortified the hill of Dargai and were impeding progress of the expedition's main column through a defile which Dargai commanded. On 18 October 1897 the 3rd Gurkhas, losing only two dead and eleven wounded, had taken the position with some ease, but withdrawn immediately because of a misunderstanding. Then,

* *The Campaign in Tirah, 1897-98* (Macmillan, 1898).

two days later, the order was given to correct the error—
and costly it was to prove. This time the Afridis were ready
and had a plan. They would hold their fire until the
attackers were exposed, charging across a 500-yard stretch
of open ground at the other side of which a steep goat-track,
providing reasonable cover, led up to the peak. This they
did to deadly effect, but Gurkhas were not to be intimidated
by such head-on danger. Led by Lieutenant A. B. Tillard
and his Scouts, riflemen of the 1/2nd and 1/3rd Gurkhas
defied the Afridis to do their worst, rushed the open ground
and found cover. Gallant but futile follow-up rushes by
more Gurkhas and British troops of the Dorsets and
Derbys failed, more than a hundred men lying dead and
dying in the open ground.

It was now that those trusted old frontier friends and
comrades of the Gurkhas, the Gordon Highlanders, were
ordered up from the rear, together with the 3rd Sikhs. As
the Gurkhas, who had scrambled on to the goat-track in
the first rush, crouched in such cover as they could find
beneath the Dargai peak, hoping that some troops would
manage to join them, there echoed through the hills a sound
which overwhelmed the beating of Afridi drums and stirred
the blood of every man in the British force. The pipers of
the Gordon Highlanders were playing 'The Cock of the
North'. Then Colonel Mathias of the Gordons addressed
his men: 'Highlanders! The general says the position must
be taken at all costs.' And the Gordons charged, accompanied by Gurkhas, Sikhs, Dorsets and Derbys, the pipers
playing the men head-on into Afridi fire.

The Gordons had assured victory. But it was Tillard and
his Gurkha Scouts who were first on the top of the hill of
Dargai and who, driving the Afridis out of the position,
enabled the British force to march through the defile and
on to the successful conclusion of another campaign.

Gurkha regiments had assimilated the lessons of campaigning in the Tirah, including the innovation of wearing

shorts, when in July 1900 the 1/4th was agreeably surprised
to be ordered to China. The Boxer Rebellion, as it came
to be known, aimed at getting rid of interfering foreigners,
particularly missionaries, had broken out and Gurkhas
were to form part of the China Expeditionary Force
assembled by outside powers—Britain, the United States,
Russia, France and Germany among them—to protect
their nationals and interests. The 1/4th arrived too late to
join in the relief of Peking, but the long journey was not
entirely wasted because they reached Shanghai in time for
their pipers to play 'The Flowers of the Forest' at a
cathedral service commemorating the death of Queen
Victoria. Their presence in China also served to introduce
Gurkhas to the German Army, giving it a foretaste of the
military professionalism they were to face in 1914. The
German commander of the international force was so
impressed by the Gurkhas that he mentioned them in
despatches to the Kaiser—for courageously cutting land-
mine wires with their kukris.

At Christmas 1902 there was one overriding topic throughout the Gurkha regiments and this was the all-important
question of their future. Considering Lord Roberts's
championship of an ever-expanding Gurkha Brigade, King
Edward VII's personal admiration of it and Nepal's consistent encouragement of recruiting, it might have seemed
a needless concern. But now a fresh and inscrutable factor
had been introduced with the arrival in India of Earl
Kitchener of Khartoum. How would the new commander-
in-chief, whose experience, apart from the war in South
Africa, was mostly Egyptian and who had never soldiered
with Gurkhas, look upon the brave little men? This was
the question the British officers and their ladies asked as
they celebrated Christmas in the messes of Almora and
Dehra Dun and wherever else the battalions happened to be.

Sir David Ochterlony, victor of the Nepal War which brought the Gurkhas into British service.

Field-Marshal Lord Roberts (mounted), who won the VC at the time of the Mutiny. Responsible for the Gurkha expansion programme of the late nineteenth century, he selected a Gurkha and a Gordon Highlander as supporters of his coat of arms.

Karanbahadur Rana, in his eighties, a First World War VC in retirement. He is photographed here in the village of Litung in the Gulmi district of Nepal.

Right:
As the 8th Army advanced into Tunisia, this rifleman of the 1/2nd Gurkhas paused to sharpen his kukri.

Below Left:
Gurkhas fought under General Montgomery at Alamein and played an important part in defeating the Afrika Korps in North Africa. Monty, who had so much fire power available, came to value the simple expedient of a Gurkha and his kukri in hill actions.

Below Right:
Ayo Gurkhali! **Riflemen of the 1/2nd Gurkhas charge near the Matmata hills in Tunisia, kukris held high.**

Unfit for further flying after being shot down as a Fleet Air Arm pilot over Malta, Michael Allmand joined the army. As a captain in the 3/6th Gurkhas he was posthumously awarded the VC in Burma.

Right:
Rifleman Tulbahadur Pun of the 3rd Gurkhas won the VC on the same day as Captain Allmand at Mogaung in Burma. Swinging a Bren gun from his hip he captured two Japanese machine-guns.

Below:
Bill Slim was presented with this Japanese sword by the 7th Gurkhas when he visited the troops in the Imphal area, Burma.

This Gurkha had just been in action against the Japanese in Burma when pictured by an official war photographer.

Left:
A Gurkha has been hit by shrapnel in Burma and is attended by an American Field Service volunteer.

Below:
The long and the short of it. Gurkhas and the Grenadier Guards at London's Chelsea Barracks. From time to time Gurkhas provide the guard at Buckingham Palace.

Word had passed round of Kitchener's first encounter with Gurkhas in circumstances which were quite out of context with usual Gurkha practice and not of the most suitable to impress the great man. This occurred soon after Kitchener's arrival in India in November 1902, during large-scale army manoeuvres outside Delhi. The exercises had been halted for a lunch-break, and it was at this juncture that a sharp-eyed adjutant-general noticed that Kitchener had finished his frugal sandwich and seemed restive to get on with things. But the adjutant-general, seeing that the staff's horses had not finished their food, good Indian Army officer that he was, looked around for a means of diverting the Commander-in-Chief. It so happened that Gurkhas were nearby in the very unlikely form of a detachment of mounted infantry–indeed a wholly absurd role for Gurkhas, about which strenuous complaints had already been made to headquarters. Nevertheless, Kitchener's interest had to be held somehow, and the unfortunate Gurkhas, who are certainly not nature's cavalrymen and have been described as 'probably the least equestrian race in Asia', were ordered to gallop half a mile, dismount and charge an imaginary enemy position on a mound.

The Gurkhas charged as though the King Emperor's very life depended upon it, which was as well because Kitchener equated excellence with the speed at which every order was carried out. He seemed pleased and fired a series of questions about these men, of whom he still knew very little:

'What sort of shots are they?' None better.

'Have they good eyesight?' Can see through a brick wall.

'How do they stand hardship?' They'll stand anything except abuse.

'Hm,' Kitchener grunted, 'pretty useful sort of soldier apparently.' For the time being, however, what worried the gossips was the comment 'apparently'.

'How do they stand hardship?'—They'll stand anything except abuse. Within a year riflemen of the 1/8th Gurkhas, fighting an action in blinding snow and at an altitude of 18,000 feet in Tibet, supplemented the reply given to Kitchener.

Tibet had a treaty with India, but suggestions of diplomatic flirtation between Lhasa and Moscow, of Russian arms entering Tibet and Tibetan border encroachments, had hastened an expedition. To reach the 'roof of the world' from the North-East Frontier—with snowblindness a serious hazard—had been arduous in the extreme. But, on 6 July 1904, to sortie in a snowstorm, scale a 2,000-foot cliff at Gyantse and throw off a force of Tibetans—it was this feat which set the seal on the Gurkha rifleman's reputation as the hardiest campaigner in the King Emperor's armed forces.

This challenge also brought out the best in the 1/8th's British officers, providing an example that their successors would find it hard to live up to. Scaling the cliff under such conditions had taxed the Gurkhas to the limit, but to reach the top, be hurled off and climb it again as had Lieutenant J. D. Grant, who was awarded the Victoria Cross, inspired the 1/8th to take the position. Lhasa was entered. No Russians were found and peaceful relations were established between India and Tibet.

This Tibetan experience—so cold was it that the battalion's recently acquired Maxim machine-gun's water-cooling system had to be laced with the riflemen's rum ration—certainly helped eliminate any professional reservations Kitchener may still have held about the Gurkhas. Gradually assimilating Gurkha lore, he became a powerful advocate of their services. The almost ecstatic relationship between Gurkha and British soldier, especially the hillmen's rapport with Scottish Highlanders, appealed to him too, associated as it was with his knowledge that during the time of the Boer War every man of the 2nd Gurkhas had given a day's pay to help the widows and orphans of their comrades in the Gordon Highlanders and 60th Rifles. Further, Kitchener agreed with Roberts's theme that no comparison could be made between the martial value of a regiment recruited from the Gurkhas of Nepal, or other warlike people in northern India, and regiments recruited in the south. Under Kitchener recruitment procedure was refined, to the extent that recruiting parties became highly selective about the areas from which men were picked.

The Indian Army divided Nepal into recruiting sectors with such deliberation that it was as if, in Britain, the army had decided to reject men from the Thames Valley in favour of hardier types from the Pennines; to enlist Devonians from Dartmoor and Exmoor, while sending home to Torquay or Teignmouth men born and reared in the softer districts of their county. These were the years in which the Gurkha element of the Indian Army grew into a permanent peacetime establishment comprising ten regiments of two battalions apiece. The swift expansion at the beginning of the twentieth century was achieved chiefly by incorporating Assam regiments, which had habitually recruited Gurkhas since 1828, as the 6th and 8th Gurkhas, and by raising two new regiments, the 7th and 10th, from the Kiranti tribes in eastern Nepal. Another unit, which had originated as the Fategarh levy in 1817, becoming the 63rd Bengal Native Infantry in 1824, now took the title of the 9th Gurkhas.

When Kitchener had been in India for four years it was time for him to make what had almost become the required commander-in-chief's pilgrimage to Katmandu. His somewhat bemused introduction to Gurkhas on horseback at the Delhi manoeuvres had been offset by the success of Gurkha pony cavalry in the recent Tibet expedition and by the general military excellence he found in Gurkha battalions when he inspected them. Kitchener was also much taken by the Gurkhas' love of sport. Not only did Gurkha proficiency at drill and rifle shooting please Kitchener, but he particularly approved an increasing keenness on the part of Gurkhas for football.

It was in the spirit of keeping sweet the source of such paragons of military service that Kitchener of Khartoum, with all the enthusiasm of a convert to the virtues of native troops, somewhat astonished Chandra Shamsher by announcing during his visit to Katmandu that, were serious war to come, he would be proud to command the Nepalese Army in association with Gurkhas already in British service. Gurkhas, Kitchener informed his host, were some of the Indian Army's bravest and most efficient soldiers. Eight years hence, Chandra Shamsher, that 'red hot soldier' as he had been dubbed by Lord Roberts, who had succeeded a brother as Prime Minister of Nepal shortly before Kitchener's arrival in India, was to have the opportunity to take Britain up on Kitchener's offer. But now he gladly accepted the honour of being made Honorary Colonel of the 4th Gurkhas.

Two years after welcoming Kitchener to Nepal it seemed appropriate to the honorary colonel, who was by now also a major-general in the British Army, to visit England. No leader of Nepal had made the journey across the *kala pani* —the ocean, literally the black water—since Jang Bahadur's call on Queen Victoria, and Chandra Shamsher was eager to press further his loyalty to the alliance, pledge a continuing supply of Gurkhas for the Indian Army in person to King Edward VII, foster trade, notably the unfettered import of arms and ammunition, and arrange to import modern farm implements. There was also another matter: to establish beyond any doubt British recognition of Nepal's position as a sovereign state. Chandra Shamsher, or Sir Chandra, following his investment by the King Emperor with a specially diamond-studded Grand Cross of the Order of the Bath, painstakingly inspected arms factories, the army, warships of the fleet, and achieved all the aims of his mission. In Scotland, displaying his natural flair for public relations, he spoke warmly of the campaigning camaraderie which made Gurkhas the brothers of the Scots.

On 6 May 1910, less than two years after Sir Chandra's return to Nepal, King Edward VII died, and as a salute of 101 guns thundered across Katmandu, four Gurkha officers stood watch—a vigil they were to share with the Grenadier Guards—by the catafalque of the King Emperor as he lay in state.

King George V had only reigned a year when he visited India, and he had accepted an invitation from Nepal to the inevitable tiger shoot in the Terai. Gurkhas greatly admire ability in the field and King George V assured the success of his visit by bagging no less than 21 tigers, 10 rhinos and 2 bears. He also took away a fine assortment of live animals as gifts from Nepal for the zoos of Britain. To Sir Chandra the 2,000 rifles and 5 million rounds of ammunition he received, in an exchange of gifts with the King Emperor, seemed a fair return for a few animals. There would be more elephants, tigers and leopards in the Terai, but rifles and ammunition were not so easily replaced. The animals from Nepal had not long settled down in captivity in Britain when European war put the goodwill generated by such courtesies to the supreme test.

CHAPTER SIX

On the Western Front and at Gallipoli

It was pelting with rain in Nepal when news reached Katmandu that Britain and France were at war with Germany. Bad weather never deflected a Gurkha from his duty, but the monsoon conditions of August 1914 made it an ordeal for hundreds of riflemen to rejoin their regiments. Nevertheless, as reports of the war across the *kala pani* reached the remote hillsides from which they had been recruited, Gurkhas said good-bye to their families and defied the elements in their efforts to report, though in some places they had to postpone river crossings for several days because of the raging waters.

For his part, while individual Gurkhas of the Indian Army walked to their depots from all over Nepal, Sir Chandra Shamsher, regretting how removed was Nepal's own army 'from the scene of actual conflict', addressed the British resident in Katmandu and placed 'the whole military resources of Nepal' at the King Emperor's disposal: an offer which, Sir Chandra emphasised, he made in two capacities—as Marshal of the Gurkhas and as a major-general in the British Army. As Prime Minister he also took the highly practical step of arranging *carte-blanche* religious cover in the form of special dispensation for every Gurkha sailing to Europe against loss of caste as a Hindu who crosses the *kala pani*.

Health was a further hazard to the speedy mobilisation and despatch of Gurkhas on active service. Riflemen of the 3rd Gurkhas were as fit as could be when they assembled at the Kotdwara railhead in the Terai, but during the rains the Terai, for all its seasonal reputation as a big-game paradise, positively oozed malaria. Failure of rail transport to coincide with their assembly exposed the 3rd Gurkhas to the bite of the mosquito for ten days, so that it was an exceedingly unfit regiment which crossed India by train to Karachi and embarked for Europe. However, considering the hurdles of nature, religion and health, the Indian Army could be congratulated on embarking a regiment of Gurkhas—240 of whom had been on their home hillsides on 4 August—within seven weeks of the outbreak of war in Europe. Not that each individual Gurkha or British officer saw it like that. To them it seemed that they would almost certainly arrive too late to fight, a prospect which, as they sailed from Karachi in September 1914, was far more dismaying than the prospect of war.

The convoy of transports carrying the Lahore and Meerut divisions of the Indian Corps to Europe heaved slowly to Suez, navigated the canal, and resumed to Malta. Only when each ship, packed with Gurkhas, Garhwal, Jat, Pathan, Sikh and British troops in such cramped conditions that not every man could find space to sleep at the same time, reached Malta, was it permitted for them to make the utmost speed individually to Marseilles. And only then did Gurkha spirits revive, all ranks regaining confidence that now they might get to the war in time. What the men of the Indian Corps did not know was that they had come half-way across the world to provide the only stopgap that Britain could muster to bolster its already worn-out and much diminished Expeditionary Force until the Territorial Army of civilians in uniform had been equipped, trained and shipped across the Channel.

Marseilles bewildered the Gurkhas. An emotional

welcome from the French seemed somewhat premature, considering that the kukris they had sharpened on the journey were still in their scabbards. The cobblestone streets seemed to have been specially laid down to make a torture of marching, while the winter underwear with which they had been issued was so incomprehensible that they wore it outside their uniforms. Once the Gurkhas had discovered the correct use for warm underwear, Marseilles housewives complained of a shortage of safety-pins. The Gurkhas had cornered the market to hold their pants up. Military muddle, it soon became clear, was not the mono-poly of the Indian Army planners who had delivered the 2/3rd Gurkhas to the certainty of malaria en route.

At Marseilles, where it was raining heavily, the Gurkha camp was a quagmire in a hollow and, as the riflemen marched in, no tents had been provided. However, such shortcomings were a realistic preparation for the far worse conditions that the men from the hills of Nepal were to encounter when they reached the front line at the end of October. It was only when they arrived at the Western Front that the seriousness of the allied situation came home to the officers of the two Indian divisions. Unaccustomed to damp cold, mud-clogged trenches and trench warfare, their native troops were expected to hold a line where British regulars had borne the brunt of weeks of attack by an enemy superior in numbers, equipped with better weapons and supplied more liberally with ammunition. Worse, they were never less than 300 yards from, and often within a grenade-throw of, everything the German Army could hurl at them. Nor were they granted rehearsal-time under operational conditions, simply because the Indian Corps had, as noted, arrived at the eleventh hour to plug a gap—to save a breakthrough which could secure a German victory on the continent within weeks.

In the autumn of 1914 the British Army held about one-tenth of the allied line, and of this, as they took up their positions, the Indian Army was responsible for about one-third. On its first day in the line, and within hours of taking up its position on 29 October, the 2nd Battalion of the 8th Gurkhas had lost six of its ten British officers killed, with three wounded. In addition, five Gurkha officers and 206 non-commissioned officers and riflemen were killed, wounded or missing. Such heavy casualties suffered by the Gurkhas on their first day in action might suggest that conditions of the Western Front had negated years of experience and tradition accumulated on the North-West Frontier. This was not so. Circumstances could not have been more different, nor had Gurkhas previously faced the heavy-gun and howitzer shellfire such as the enemy brought down upon their trenches. Yet they continued to counter-attack, with ever-increasing casualties, their bravery astonishing the German infantry and calling forth the cheers of British comrades.

Gurkhas had not been in the line many hours when the dreadful truth hit their surviving British officers: that the Gurkhas, remainder of the Indian Corps and the cut-to-ribbons British Expeditionary Force, represented all there was in their sector to stem a tidal wave of German divisions seeking a breakthrough. In the late autumn of 1914 there were no reserves, and there would be none until first the Territorial Army, and later Kitchener's new armies of drilled civilians, arrived. Nor would there be respite until Germany withdrew divisions from the west to counter Russian pressure. The location of the Indian Corps was along a line from Givenchy, some 5 miles east of Béthune to Rouges Banc, just south of Armentières. Along this line the Lahore and Meerut divisions had relieved the 2nd British Corps.

To the little hillmen some of the trenches vacated by taller British troops presented a particular problem. Keeping the average European soldier knee-deep in mud and water, they almost swallowed up a Gurkha, and several riflemen were drowned before they had fired a shot. In many trenches Gurkhas, unable to see over the parapets, had to improvise makeshift platforms from the bric-a-brac of trench life.

On 12 November Lord Roberts, unwilling even at the age of eighty-two to be separated for long from his beloved Gurkhas and now Colonel of the 5th Gurkhas, visited the front line. It was said that the veteran field-marshal from India had drafted King George V's message to the Indian Corps: 'You will be the first Indian soldiers of the King Emperor who will have the honour of showing in Europe that the sons of India have lost none of their ancient martial instincts . . . you are the descendants of men who have been great rulers and great warriors. . . .' But in the damp and cold and mud of the November battlefield it grieved the old soldier to observe the recipients of that exhortation—successors of the men who had marched with him from Kabul to the relief of Kandahar—bogged down, drowning in their trenches, short of ammunition, unnaturally on the defensive, and denied the opportunity of their normal instinct to draw kukris, to advance and to keep advancing. They told the old campaigner from India how, ten days earlier, a number of men of the 2nd Battalion, the 2nd Gurkhas, had been blown to kingdom-come near the village of Neuve-Chapelle; and of the surprise the Germans had when, assuming that no enemy could survive their artillery barrage and fight back, an infantry charge was repulsed by some twelve Gurkhas and a young British lieutenant in hand-to-hand fighting, in which kukri clashed with bayonet and rifles were swung by their barrels, the heavy butts crashing into the jaws of the enemy. And as Roberts listened he must have seen again in his mind's eye the Sirmoor Battalion, forerunner of the 2nd Gurkhas, defending Hindu Rao's House on the Ridge at Delhi during the Mutiny, and he knew that the Gurkha had not changed, only the conditions to which he was beginning to adapt himself.

Roberts heard how, with the help of the 1/9th, repeated charges by the 2/2nd had so demoralised the German infantry that it yielded the gains which shellfire had largely won for it; the 2/2nd losing 31 dead with more than 100 'missing'—as was said of men in 1914, almost all of whom were as dead as the body count and were never seen again.

Two days later Lord Roberts, the strain and the cold too much for old bones which had spent forty-one years in India, collapsed and died. It was a French general who, acknowledging the field-marshal's death in a general order, found the appropriate words for a tribute. 'Lord Roberts', wrote General de Maud'Huy, 'has died in an hour of mighty battles in the midst of the troops which he loved so well.'

Towards the end of December the Indian Corps was withdrawn for a rest, although for the Gurkha element it was more of a working holiday serving the same purpose. The riflemen marched and marched about the French countryside in the safety of rear areas to harden feet withered by trench conditions. Together with reinforcements, they also carried out training exercises which their hasty October committal had denied them.

The New Year was but two weeks of age when the Gurkhas returned to the trenches, but it was almost early spring before their special qualities were employed in an offensive. Large-scale German withdrawals to counter the Russians had thinned out the enemy infantry, offering an invitation to the Allies to pick a battleground, concentrate troops in superior numbers and go forward. So far as the Gurkhas were concerned this battleground was in the area of the village of Neuve-Chapelle, which at this stage was again in German hands. At last Gurkhas were to play their natural game. They were on the attack and they responded with all the will and aggression of men who were set upon avenging their dead and justifying the reputation that had preceded them from India. Here at Neuve-Chapelle in March 1915 Gurkhas attached fresh glory to their warrior reputation, and it was almost as if each man had determined to reply to the King Emperor's message through the example of his personal conduct. Eight months of war on the Western Front had produced countless deeds of courage, but Havildar Bahadur Thapa's rushing of a barricade with a handful of men, his killing of sixteen German soldiers and capture of two machine-guns, deeds for which he was awarded the Indian Order of Merit, set a high standard, even for Gurkhas.

In the same engagement, Rifleman Gane Gurung, determined to silence a hail of fire from a fortified house, charged straight at the position as fast as his short brown legs could carry him. When he was next seen the firing had ceased and eight Germans were being marched into captivity at the point of the Gurkha's bayonet. While from the King Emperor Rifleman Gane Gurung was to receive the Indian Order of Merit, from the British troops who had observed his feat there came an immediate and spontaneous acclamation. Three cheers for the Gurk, shouted one of their number and the hip, hip, hurrays could be heard by the astonished Germans.

Earlier, as massed artillery of 450 guns and howitzers prepared for the initiative, the cheers would have been inaudible. British officers of the 3rd Gurkhas said it was like standing under a railway bridge over which thousands of express trains were passing at lightning speed. To the Gurkhas it was beyond description. There was no sound in their experience with which they could compare a sustained artillery barrage of such intensity. All they knew was that some of the shell and splinter intended for the enemy seemed to fall short. For how, in the apparent absence of German shelling, had one of their number just lost his head?

If by May 1915 the novelty of Gurkhas and other 'brown

rascals' of the Indian Corps, as the Germans called them, had worn off, there was still a certain incongruity about Gurkhas from Nepal achieving a reputation on a European battlefield equalled only by that of the Brigade of Guards. Nor did the incongruity stop there. The very names of the formations in whose orders Gurkha battalions appeared were wholly out of context with Givenchy, Neuve-Chapelle, Armentieres, Ypres, as is borne out by a short extract from the Garhwal Brigade Operation Order No 49, of May 1915: 'Meerut division is to deliver the attack . . . artillery of the Meerut division reinforced by that of the Lahore division. . . . The Dehra Dun brigade is to assault the enemy's front line trenches'—and it did, but the enemy got wind of the plan and it was a costly failure.

Summer came, but the weariness of the war of attrition strained the smiles greeting the sun that Gurkhas had missed so much through the first winter of war. The riflemen found such relief as they could in dredging humour from the sight of one another wearing the primitive, grotesque gas-masks which had been issued to protect them in the gas warfare initiated by the Germans. The masks appealed to the Gurkhas' ever-ready sense of the ridiculous and ability to laugh at themselves.

Among their British officers, who were predominantly from the public school reservoir of leaders for service in the British Empire, the sunshine stirred memories of happier times—of polo and pigsticking in India, and of earlier schooldays and cricket in England. There were Wykehamists in the 2nd Battalion, the 3rd Gurkhas, and they put down their commanding officer's keen eye to his ability as a catch, remembering, to Lieutenant-Colonel Vincent Ormsby's pleasure, how as a schoolboy he had won Winchester's annual Lord's match against Eton in 1883 with a superb catch to dismiss the last man in. In August 1915, when the battalion occupied a section of the line north of Neuve-Chapelle, the Wykehamists named their headquarters Winchester Farm and here Colonel Ormsby and his adjutant, Captain Tuite-Dalton, another Wykehamist, carved their names on an oak board as though it were a school scholarships roll of honour. When the war was over the board, and two others, commemorated more than thirty Wykehamists who had passed this way. For Ormsby it was a memorial. He was dead.

There was no laughter as Gurkhas of the 2/3rd and 2/8th pulled gas-masks over their faces in the early hours of 25 September. This was the day set for the Loos offensive and for the first British use of poison gas. This day, in place of the earlier smiles that had greeted the issue of gas-masks, there were expressions of concern and dismay that riflemen had been gassed before the alarm was given. Not only had an unfavourable wind blown gas across British trenches, but a fluke hit by an enemy mortar had released gas from other cylinders. This meant that at 6 am as the 2/3rd Gurkhas went forward over the parapets of their trenches they were disadvantaged by wearing masks to protect them from their own side's gas. To add to the discomfort their own smokescreen had been turned into a dense fog by the damp air of the early morning, reducing visibility to a few yards. Then, as if they were not already the victims of enough troubles of their own side's making, they reached the enemy front line only to find that the preliminary bombardment had failed to break down the barbed-wire defences.

The result was disastrous. The Gurkhas, emerging from the thick fog, came right up against the wire and into the face of murderous rifle- and machine-gun fire. They had no option but to range along the wire in search of gaps. Most of those who found openings were gunned down as they attempted to struggle through. Of the 2/3rd only Lieutenant T. P. Wood and four men managed to fight their way through the wire and into an enemy trench, where Wood and three riflemen died in hand-to-hand fighting. Afterwards 35 Gurkha bodies were counted lying on top of the German parapet and the wire was hung with many more of the 2/3rd's 100 dead and 131 wounded. Among the dead were three British officers, including a lieutenant-colonel.

It may be wondered what became of the sole survivor of Lieutenant Wood's small party. Somehow in the fury of the morning Rifleman Kulbir Thapa survived, got beyond the first trench and stumbled into a wounded private of the 2nd Leicesters. Realising that the Gurkha had a chance of saving himself the English soldier implored him to leave, but Kulbir remained and comforted the wounded man for the rest of the day and through the following night. Then, under cover of an early morning mist, he manhandled the private across the trench, through the wire, and into the comparative safety of a shell-hole. After two more trips to retrieve wounded Gurkhas from the wire, Kulbir began to carry the Leicesters' private back to the British lines. By now, however, the mist had lifted and the Germans concentrated heavy fire on the diminutive Gurkha until the very moment he reached the trenches of the Garhwal Rifles and delivered his English comrade to their immediate care.

During his visit to Nepal in 1911 King George V had made the gesture that Gurkhas would henceforth be eligible for the Victoria Cross. Rifleman Kulbir Thapa of the 2/3rd was the first Gurkha to win one.

Just how many Victoria Crosses were earned that day? It will never be known because so few survived to tell the tale, Kulbir's award owing much to the recommendations of onlookers from the 39th Garhwals and 2nd Leicesters. Possibly one more at least was deserving of a member of the 2/8th Gurkhas, whose experience had been no less harrowing than that of Kulbir's battalion. Yet missing out as they did on the supreme award the 2/8th were not

without their trophies, Riflemen Bahadur Pun and Rat-
baran Gurung returning with a German machine-gun
apiece. But the battalion's losses were out of all proportion
to the value of such acquisitions. Of some 500 of the 2/8th
who had contributed to the early morning attack on 25
September, one British officer, one Gurkha officer and 49
riflemen were all it could muster at sunset. Nor was
Lieutenant-Colonel G. M. Morris, the commanding
officer, available to succour the survivors or make recommendations for gallantry, for he was among the dead. The
battalion which, as it sailed from India, had worried that it
might arrive in Europe too late to fight, had all but
disappeared.

'Better to die than be coward. . . .' They had died along
the German wire with this Gurkha saying on their lips, each
man contented that he had given of his best, and uncom-
prehendingly as the enemy saw it, for a King Emperor who
was not their ruler and a country to which they did not
belong. Of 200,000 Gurkhas who left hill villages in Nepal
to fight for the British Empire in the First World War,
20,000 were to die, loyal to the end to a land most of them
had never seen. Ordinarily, only the wounded from France
had the opportunity of satisfying the Gurkha rifleman's
curiosity about England, London, and in the capital, Tower
Bridge—'the bridge that breaks in half,' as the wounded
described it. The strength of this curiosity became apparent
when a party of 3rd Gurkha wounded, finding themselves
not in London but in Hampshire in the New Forest,
complained, 'We are now convalescent and were promised
we should see London. What, then, are we doing in this
jungle?' Henceforth, visits were arranged.

In November 1915 the survivors of the Meerut and
Lahore divisions marched out of the front line. They had
filled a gap while Kitchener's new armies of civilian volunteers were recruited, uniformed and drilled, and now they
were needed just as urgently elsewhere.

The rugged Gallipoli peninsula might have been land-scaped as the ideal military proving-ground for Gurkha qualities. No senior British officer appreciated this better than General Sir Ian Hamilton who commanded the Expeditionary Force which, in April 1915, sought with naval support to force the straits of the Dardanelles and open a supply route to allied Russia. Other than the prac-tical issue of supplying Russia, Britain hoped to stage a successful initiative which would counter public disillusion over the bogged-down situation in France and to relieve the Russian Army by drawing off Turkish troops against whom it was engaged in the Caucasus.

As a young officer Hamilton had served under Roberts and observed the 5th Gurkhas in action in Afghanistan. Requesting Gurkhas from Kitchener he called attention to the 'scrubby hillsides' of the terrain where 'these little fellows are at their brilliant best'. At Gallipoli, the general opined, 'Each little Gurk might be worth his full weight in gold'.

In summary, Gallipoli developed into a series of naval and military planning disasters for which no blame attached to the men who had to do the fighting and from which the Gurkhas emerged, as Hamilton had known they would, with much glory.

When the 1/6th Gurkhas landed on 1 May 1915, five days after the assault had started, the British, Australian and New Zealand components of the Expeditionary Force were still on the beach-heads and suffering heavy casualties from the fire of the Turkish defenders, the sheer cliffs and heights having pulled the invaders up short. There was, however, just one hope, and this was that the Turkish right flank could be attacked by the scaling and taking of a 300-foot cliff from which machine-gun posts prohibited all possible advance. This was warfare more in keeping with Gurkha qualities and experience than had been offered by the terrain and conditions in France. Where two Irish regiments had failed, the Gurkhas took the position and beat off counter-attacks with such rapid, continuous and accurate rifle-fire that the woodwork of many of their rifles blistered from the heat as 2,000 Turks died in a rush against the Gurkha lines. Afterwards Hamilton gave a name to that Turkish cliff and it was entered on maps and charts as Gurkha Bluff.

Despite the cumulative naval and military catastrophes associated with it, the Gallipoli campaign provides a setting for an account of Gurkha participation that to some extent mitigates the whole sorry affair; a setting in which, as the summer of 1915 progressed and so much went wrong, Gurkha battalions surpassed themselves, their main contribution centring on the narrow neck of the isthmus which joins the Aegean Sea peninsula to the mainland.

In early June General Sir Ian Hamilton exchanged two Punjabi battalions of the 29th Indian Brigade for the 1/5th and 2/10th Gurkhas. This was not because of doubts about Punjabi valour but because it was considered impolitic to send Moslem soldiers into battle against Turks. Each Gurkha battalion was soon involved in heavy fighting and severe losses. Casualties reached proportions commonplace on the Western Front and, stalemate trench warfare setting in, often for similar reasons. The 1/6th, an advance pulled up sharply by wire which was supposed to have been cleared by artillery fire, lost 95 men in not many more seconds. The same day the 1/5th lost 129, including 7 British officers. The fighting in June produced a host of memorable incidents. Naik Dhan Singh Gurung, twice captured, made two escapes, on the second occasion hurling himself into the sea in full equipment and swimming under fire to a friendly beach. A British officer was shot dead brandishing his sword as he led a Gurkha kukri charge. Another British officer, badly wounded and suffering from brain damage, could only speak Gurkhali for the few weeks he lingered on. . . .

When the Indian brigade was withdrawn locally on 9 July the three Gurkha battalions had lost more than a thousand men between them in killed or wounded.

On the night of 6 August the Gurkhas returned, and it was now, in a war in which so many tragedies resulted from avoidable errors, that there occurred a tragedy of immeasurable consequences.

Of the three major heights which dominated the peninsula from the spine connecting Suvla Bay and the Dardanelles one 1,000-foot peak, Sari Bair, overtopped its companions. To possess this height was to obtain control of the peninsula, with the prospect of launching a drive on Istanbul, or rather Constantinople as that Turkish city was then called, and of then throwing the Turks back across the Bosporus and thus out of Europe.

After heavy fighting the 1/5th, 2/5th, 2/10th and 1/6th advanced from a Suvla Bay landing, inching their way up the slopes of Sari Bair in the face of annihilating fire. Within 500 yards of the summit the 1/6th had lost 76 men, but the Gurkhas gained another 200 yards and then fought for three days until there they were looking down on the narrows of the Dardanelles and towards the entrance to the Marmara Sea. But this was no time to admire the view or consider what lay beyond. A savage hand-to-hand battle ensued, the Gurkhas tearing into the Turks until the enemy turned and ran down the eastern slopes of the peak, leaving the Gurkhas with the key to the peninsula of Gallipoli.

It was now that tragedy in the shape of two terrible mistakes intervened. The Royal Navy, not realising that Gurkhas had replaced Turks on the summit of Sari Bair, resumed bombardment of the position—and supporting troops, who had lost their way in the night, failed to arrive. The Turks were not slow to grab the chance offered by the naval bombardment and they were further assisted in an easy recapture of the height by that most unusual event, a Gurkha retreat. Whether the Gurkhas would have attempted to hold on until the shelling error was corrected and reinforcements could arrive, had a British officer survived and made a personal decision in the field, cannot be known, but Subedar-Major Gambirsingh Pun of the 1/6th received orders to retreat and, quite correctly, he obeyed them.

In that moment the Allies lost one of the great opportunities of the First World War. For three months the campaign faltered on. The baking heat of the summer cooled through the autumn and November brought torrential rain, flooded trenches and ice and snow on the contested hillsides. The Gurkha riflemen fought on, even when lumps of ice as large and solid as refrigerator cubes formed between their toes. When they removed their boots the feet of many of the men were found to be black with gangrene from neglected frostbite. The 2/10th reported 450 cases of frostbite and many riflemen had to be invalided, maimed for life.

In these conditions Kitchener visited the peninsula. The former Commander-in-Chief, India, who was now Secretary of State for War, inspected the troops and shortly afterwards, on his recommendation, evacuation was ordered. On the night of 19 December the Gallipoli campaign was over. The last unit of Hamilton's ill-fated force to leave, the 1/5th Gurkhas, stole silently away in the night, their boots sound-proofed by blanket wrappings.

When the Gurkhas were withdrawn from France, General Sir James Willcocks, commander of the Indian Corps, said of them: 'I have now come to the conclusion that the best of my troops in France were Gurkhas . . . taciturn by nature, brave and loyal to a degree, the Gurkhas ended, as I knew they would, second to none.' At Gallipoli, for all the brave deeds of British, Australian and New Zealand troops, a young subaltern of the Royal Warwickshire Regiment was so inspired by the bearing of the Gurkhas, particularly of the 1/6th, that he decided to join them. That subaltern was Lieutenant William Slim who, as commander of the Fourteenth Army in Burma in the Second World War, might well have failed to save India from the Japanese but for the contribution of the Gurkhas.

Meantime there was another campaign to fight, hardships to endure ahead as severe as those in France and Gallipoli, and still years before Nepal invited Britain to pick the flower of its manhood for the second time in a quarter of a century.

CHAPTER SEVEN

Mesopotamia and Palestine, 1915–18

At Christmas in 1915 Suez, at the Red Sea end of the Suez Canal, where generations of British troops on passage home habitually teased eastbound troopships with shouts of 'You're going the wrong way', provided a convenient junction for Gurkha battalions; for some of which the eastbound passage was at last the 'right way'. Ashore, British officers, Gurkha officers and Gurkha other ranks, survivors of the Western Front and Gallipoli, and reinforcements fresh from India, exchanged stories of their experiences. Those who had fought the Germans and the Turks heard that some 16,000 men of the Nepalese Army had taken over their traditional duties along the North-West Frontier of India. They learned, too, that Gurkhas had beaten off the Turks in defence of the Suez Canal, and they were briefed on a campaign in Mesopotamia where Gurkha battalions were henceforth to be primarily employed, each of the ten regiments of the Gurkha Brigade being represented in the course of the campaign.

Following the failure at Gallipoli, the focus of the allied effort to destroy the Turkish Empire, in military alliance with Germany, shifted to an army which had been engaging the Turks in the plain between the Euphrates and Tigris Rivers since 6 November 1914; that is, well before the Gallipoli landings. Possession of this arid region, now Iraq, but then known as Mesopotamia—or 'Mespot' as it was called by British and Indian Army soldiers—had seemed imperative after Turkey's entry into the war. To occupy it was to safeguard Persian Gulf oil supplies and the Suez link with the Far East and to deny Germany the opportunity of opening up a land route to India.

The position early in 1915 was that after its November landing at the head of the Persian Gulf the 6th Indian Division had occupied Basra and pushed forward to a point some 60 miles from the Gulf where the Euphrates and Tigris join to make the Shatt-al-Arab. Ahead, across 500 miles of monotonous, treeless, almost waterless country offering no cover in temperatures climbing to 120°F in the shade, glittered what appeared from that distance to be the tantalising city of Baghdad. Far removed from the flies, malaria, cholera, smallpox, dysentery and heat-strokes of Mesopotamia, a British cabinet, chastened by Gallipoli and needing a success, set its sights on the city of the *Arabian Nights*. Viewed from Westminster the capture of Baghdad and the opening of this route to the heart of Turkey was feasible. Certainly in the spring, summer and autumn of 1915 while the Turks were preoccupied with Gallipoli, Baghdad would be at its most vulnerable.

Another Indian division had arrived in Mesopotamia and, of its number, the 2/7th Gurkhas made a swift impact. In a remarkable advance, Gurkhas clearing the way with kukri charges wherever impeded by Turkish resistance, a British force under Major-General Sir Charles Townshend fought its way in late November to the ruins of the ancient city of Ctesiphon, only 25 miles from Baghdad. However, Townshend's 12,000-strong force had expended itself. It was in no shape to press on to Baghdad. In the face of growing resistance from 20,000 Turkish infantry it fell back 80 miles to Kut on the Tigris. But first, to cover the retreat and provide time for the preparation of defensive positions within the walls of Kut, Gurkhas fought one of the most celebrated actions of their story. At Gallipoli they were already commemorated by a cliff renamed Gurkha Bluff, and now in Mesopotamia Gurkhas were to stand and die on a hillock which was henceforth known as Gurkha Mound.

Townshend had lost more than one-third of his force in the fighting at Ctesiphon when 300 Gurkhas of the 2/7th and 100 Punjabis moved on to the Mound and awaited the attentions of a Turkish division several thousand strong. Then in the early evening the Turks came forward, thousands of them against 400 men armed with rifles and supported by one Maxim machine-gun battery. Yet, such was the discipline of the Gurkhas and Punjabis, that they controlled their fire so tightly that, as the night wore on, each successive wave of yelling Turks was shattered and prevented from overwhelming the Mound by weight of numbers. At dawn the Turks had gone and, thanks to the stand on Gurkha Mound, Townshend was enabled to make an orderly retreat. He entered Kut on 3 December 1915, prepared for a siege, and there he awaited relief.

Their fellow-countrymen locked up in Kut, Gurkhas of the 1/2nd, 1/8th and 1/9th fought hard to reach them. They suffered heavy casualties and much hardship, but the Turks had moved strong reinforcements of Gallipoli-experienced troops to Mesopotamia. On 29 April 1916, his force out of rations and reduced by disease, Townshend surrendered.

Conditions for prisoners of the Turks were deplorable and Gurkhas, who had defended Gurkha Mound with their saying 'Better to die than be a coward' on their lips, made unhappy occupants of prisoner-of-war compounds. However, repeating to themselves just as they did when gravely wounded, 'I am a Gurkha, I must not cry out', they put a good face on captivity and maintained such remarkable standards of military discipline that the Turks improved conditions out of sheer admiration for their general bearing.

Despite the failure at heavy cost of two relief forces the vision of an occupied Baghdad continued to mesmerise the British Government and, in all, 600,000 troops were to be committed to the Mesopotamian campaign. But the politicians were far removed from the conditions, in which supplies were so poor that Gurkha riflemen had to make trousers from sackcloth, and climate and disease rivalled the Turk as an enemy. In a Gallipoli winter Gurkhas had fought with ice in their boots. In Mesopotamia the dust and the sand burnt the soles of their feet through their boots.

In August 1916 improvements began under a new commander, Lieutenant-General Sir Stanley Maude, and bemused Gurkha audiences were shown Charlie Chaplin films sent out from London for the good of their morale, although they were to get a bigger laugh from the army's latest issue gas-mask. It had a nose-clip but, try as he might, the average Mongolian-featured Gurkha could not adjust it to his squat nose.

In the new year of 1917 Maude's force, which included a freshly formed 2/7th Battalion, fighting from river bend to river bend, gradually pushed the Turks back up the Tigris, and it was at Shumran Bend during these operations that Major Wheeler of the 2/9th won the Victoria Cross.

On 11 March 1917 the 2/4th were among the first of Maude's troops to march into Baghdad. To the Gurkhas the city of the *Arabian Nights* was just another milestone of a war in which they were fighting as professional soldiers and had no other object than to bring honour upon their people and their regiment. There were, however, those among their British officers who, observing the looting by Arabs, the dead animals, the diseased and half-starved dogs in the streets, could not but wonder that so much had been endured to gain such a god-awful place.

Baghdad, once achieved, was regarded as a staging-post for a push further north towards Mosul and Turkey. Half-way there, at Tekrit, Maude himself contracted cholera and died. His death coincided with a reluctant acceptance that the drain of prolonged trench warfare on the Western Front had rendered the Mesopotamian campaign insupportable. As with old soldiers who never die, it simply faded away in favour of a developing offensive in Palestine where Gurkhas were already much involved in opening another road to Turkey by way of Jerusalem, Damascus and Aleppo.

The fight to expel the Turks from the Palestinian and Syrian extremes of their empire was exercising the army of General Sir Edmund Allenby to the limit when Gurkhas appeared on the scene. At first they were greeted with some scepticism, because wholly unfounded stories were rife that the little hillmen were among Indian troops withdrawn from France because they had been a liability. British officers of Gurkha battalions in Palestine, while angered by the rumours, knew that given the chance to get at the Turks and their German allies who had arrived to bolster them, the Gurkhas would very soon show that they were second to none, as was usual wherever they fought.

Some 30 miles beyond Gaza, in early November, as Allenby's troops drove the Turks northwards, resistance stiffened and the Gurkhas were offered an ideal opportunity to confound the misinformed gossip. As at Dargai in the Tirah campaign some twenty years earlier, a well-defended hill position impeded the advance and, as at Dargai, a first assault which included British troops had failed to hold its ground. Now at Brown Hill the 1/4th Royal Scots were thrown off the slopes by a Turkish counter-attack and the defences were swiftly strengthened with machine-guns.

Soon after, the 2/3rd Gurkhas and 2/5th Hampshires were ordered to make a frontal attack and the Gurkhas, eager to get among the Turks, reported their readiness. But the Hampshires took their time and Lieutenant-Colonel C. S. Eastmead of the 2/3rd felt obliged to complain to the brigadier on behalf of his riflemen that the Hampshires were letting the side down. The Gurkhas had to contain their ardour for two hours and twenty minutes before the Hampshires were ready for battle. When at last the order to advance was given the Gurkha and the English battalion, under cover from South Africa artillery, moved forward and on to an open plain. A mile away the Turks awaited them on the hill from which they had previously repulsed the Royal Scots.

Long years of experience in India told the Gurkhas that they had got to get across the open ground as quickly as they could, but now the Hampshires, slow off the mark from the very start, lagged behind, crossing the plain in fits and starts as they made frequent halts to fire their rifles. Meanwhile, the Gurkhas, brushing aside losses, including Lieutenant H. L. Rennison, their machine-gun officer, as they advanced rapidly into enemy shell- and machine-gun fire, reached the shelter of the dry bed of a river some 200 yards below the top of Brown Hill. Here they found the remnants of the Royal Scots who, rallied by the arrival of the 2/3rd Gurkhas, joined them in a bayonet charge which carried the summit, where a great pile of dead bodies of Turks and Royal Scots testified to the struggle which had taken place in the earlier attempt.

If the action at Brown Hill confounded the misinformed detractors of the Indian Army, another incident served to upset critics of the kukri's value as a weapon and of the 2 pounds 14 ounces it added to the 54-pound 13-ounce load carried in action. Summoned for the good of their education to observe the demolition of a cactus hedge of a type which could present an awkward obstacle to an advance, a party of riflemen was instructed that gun-cotton blast would provide the answer. However, after a noisy explosion the hedge remained impenetrable. Smiling all over their faces the hillmen moved in with drawn kukris and swiftly carved the required gap.

Thus, in Palestine, had the curving blade described by Gillespie's dragoons at Kalunga some hundred years earlier as a farm implement, come full circle. All the more remarkable was the fact that some recently issued kukris were of curious manufacture. Hard put to equip more than 2,000 recruits trained there, a depot at Maymo in Burma had overcome the problem by establishing its own kukri works and forging the weapon from carriage springs discarded by the railway shops and improvising a scabbard of jungle timber and goatskin leather.

Improvisation, ingenuity, making do, such were the imperatives in Allenby's army as, progressively starved of men by the demand of the front in France, and parched and never certain of its water supplies, it nevertheless enforced the Turkish abandonment of Jerusalem on 8 December 1917, and then pushed ever forward, ever northward. 'No praise is too high for these brilliant and frugal operations', Winston Churchill wrote in tribute. But such tributes, made in retrospect and far removed from the heat of the day, inevitably bypass the minutiae of the hard toil and petty irritations endured in a prolonged campaign in a difficult climate. No British officer commanding Gurkhas in Palestine in the summer of 1918 was likely to forget, for instance, the anger at the authorities' apparent indifference to the pride taken by riflemen in their distinctive Kashmir felt hats. 'Unobtainable' came the persistent reply as battalions indented for hats lost on active service, and yet similar hats were being issued to empire troops. Nor on their return to Nepal were Gurkhas to forget the strenuous pick-and-shovel postscript to each Palestinian encounter as they buried their own dead and heaped soil and sand over the bones of the countless German soldiers who had died so far away from the fatherland.

Bury the dead after the battle and fight again next day. It was routine, but routine interspersed with heroic moments which were to add to the ever-expanding Gurkha legend. And almost as routine was the presence of machine-gun nests which invited the attentions of potential VCs. Near El Kefr, north of Jerusalem, after several attempts to occupy the flat top of a ridge had been rendered fruitless and costly by machine-gun fire from a position across open ground, Lieutenant F. Barter of the 2/3rd Gurkhas, who was already a VC, and Jemadar Budhibal Thapa, holder of the Military Cross, decided that between them they must not merely silence the German-manned machine-gun but capture it—for so prized a trophy had thus far eluded Jemadar Budhibal, who had set his heart on it. Accompanied by a handful of riflemen the British and Gurkha officers made their charge, but they fared no better than their predecessors. Budhibal and every rifleman in the party died in the open ground, only Barter surviving the onslaught. For five hours he lay motionless, feigning death, only 30 yards from the barrel of the enemy machine-gun.

It was now that Rifleman Karanbahadur Rana and a small party, taking a Lewis gun with them, crept stealthily forward with the object of fighting it out, machine-gun to machine-gun, in a duel across the flat top of the Palestinian ridge. Yet, within seconds of opening fire, the Lewis gunner was killed. Quickly Karanbahadur heaved his dead comrade off the machine-gun and, undaunted by the hail of fire directed at him as well as by hand-grenades lobbed from the enemy position, knocked out the German machine-gun crew and continued to fire until he had silenced the enemy rifle-fire and grenade attacks. Were all this not sufficient to qualify the Gurkha rifleman for the VC, he yet managed, when on two occasions the Lewis gun jammed, coolly to remedy the stoppages. Karanbahadur's action also resulted in the rescue of Lieutenant Barter.

It was through such acts of 'conspicuous bravery, resource in action under adverse conditions and utter contempt of danger', as the War Office citation recorded Karanbahadur's Victoria Cross, that Allenby was enabled to continue north until finally the Turks were defeated. They were obliged to sign an armistice on 31 October 1918-the Germans following suit within two weeks.

Armistice did not bring peace to the Gurkha regiments, since inevitably the aftermath of such a disruptive war left various pockets of trouble. In June 1918 an emergency force of Gurkhas was moved in 300 Ford vans and light lorries over the Peitak pass to Resht on the Caspian Sea to rescue the British consul who was besieged in his smouldering building by rebel tribesmen. Gurkhas remained in the region for three years, their presence being particularly opportune, saving as it did Persia from Russian communist or Turkish domination. Gurkhas were also used to put down an Arab rebellion in Iraq.

Back in their traditional 'peace-time' campaigning area of the North-West Frontier they soon demonstrated that neither France, Palestine nor Mesopotamia had blunted their expertise in or appeased their appetite for mountain warfare. When in 1919 Nasrullah Khan murdered his brother the Amir, seized power in Afghanistan and attempted to invade India at the head of the Khyber Pass each Gurkha regiment was represented by a battalion. Nepal, as if making a point of recognising that the World War was over and frontier life returning to normal, sent 2,000 troops of its own to help. Well, almost to normal. Nobody involved in this campaign was very pleased, be he Afridi, Gurkha or Briton, that the Afghan ruler had chosen unsportingly to go to war in May with weeks of bakingly hot weather ahead.

The Amir was defeated, but there were many incidents in the interim to alert frontier tribes to the fact that neither the British Raj nor its punitive instrument, the Gurkha battalion, had lost its touch. One such incident captures the spirit that imbued each individual rifleman in this sunset period of the British Empire. A fort at Thal was under Afghan siege when its flag halyards were shot away, the Union Jack making an undignified, crumpled descent to earth. This was an affront that was more than a young Gurkha of the 3/9th could stand. Disregarding nearby and accurate sniper-fire the little hillman shinned up the flag-staff and nailed the Union Jack firmly back in place.

Another portent that life had returned to normal was the arrival in the Terai during December 1921 of the Prince of Wales—later King Edward VIII and Duke of Windsor—to enjoy, as had his father and grandfather, a lavishly mounted hunting expedition.

Apart from keeping the riflemen fit and trained the frontier troubles of the inter-war years provided useful experience of command at all levels for British officers and it helped freshly appointed subalterns to get to know their men and their customs under active service conditions which were not necessarily so formal as in the regimental depots. There was, however, one custom which, while it was observed where possible on active service, could only be done justice amid home station comforts and facilities. This was the Gurkha soldier's festival of Dushera. The Hindu festival marks the opening of the cold-weather season following the rains. Lasting ten days and featuring aspects of a harvest festival, its Gurkha ceremonies dwell on the honouring of Durga, the Goddess of War, thus refreshing martial instincts for the coming year and hoping to guarantee, battalion by battalion, good fortune in battle and all activities. Superstition dictates that such fortune depends on the competence of one of their number despatching a sacrifice, preferably a tethered buffalo, with a single decapitating blow of an oversized kukri-type weapon which is almost a sword in appearance. If a battalion was destined for the frontier after the festival the sacrificial ceremony was followed with particular interest. Another important ritual is the blessing of weapons, not merely the simple kukri, but in modern times the rifle and machine-gun, to the accompaniment of suitable hymns:

> Great Goddess, Mother Durga,
> We thank thee, mistress of the world,
> We offer up flowers and leaves,
> We the brave race of Gurkhas.*

The soldier's festival was observed with especial fervour in October 1940, because Gurkhas were about to cross the *kala pani* and to fight overseas again.

* *Johnny Gurkha* (Robert Hale, 1964).

CHAPTER EIGHT

Ayo Gurkhali!—Here Come the Gurkhas!

'Of course'. Tersely and without consulting the council around him, Sir Judha Shamsher, brother of Sir Chandra, who had authorised Britain's use of Gurkhas in the First World War, acceded the formal request for Gurkhas of the Indian Army to serve again overseas as Lieutenant-Colonel Geoffrey Betham, Britain's resident minister, stood before him in Katmandu. The brevity of the Prime Minister of Nepal's response reflected a recognition of urgency and also a certain impatience over the lateness of the request. As with his revered predecessor Jang Bahadur at the time of the Mutiny, and his brother Sir Chandra in 1914, Sir Judha had anticipated Britain's need and offered assistance as early as 1938 when he regarded the appeasement of Germany as inevitably leading to another world war.

Nearly two years had passed since Sir Judha had offered eight battalions of the Nepalese Army for service in India, and now it was the summer of 1940. France had fallen without a Gurkha present to fight alongside British troops, as in 1914, or to share the perils of the Dunkirk beaches and the evacuation. Nor had Gurkhas crossed the *kala pani* to help protect Britain's oil supplies in the Middle East or to bolster the island's meagre defences as it awaited the invasion which, from remote Katmandu, seemed likely in 1940.

Once Nepal's agreement to overseas service had been given it was the British minister's duty to seek permission for the expansion of the Gurkha element of the Indian Army. As readily and with a further 'of course' Sir Judha approved the raising of a third and fourth battalion for each of the ten regiments and the formation of a battalion—in the event there were two battalions—of paratroop volunteers. The alacrity and generosity of Nepal's response and its prime minister's personal displeasure at the tardiness of Britain's request were all the more remarkable considering the rising tide of Indian nationalism and the excuse for a lesser degree of co-operation the Himalayan kingdom could have offered in an understandable unwillingness to upset its powerful freedom-seeking neighbour. There was also the problem, as Colonel Betham was only too well aware as he stood before Sir Judha, that the council numbered its doubters on the chances of Britain's survival, not least among them General Padma Shamsher, the Prime Minister's nephew. But Sir Judha restricted the occasion to a formal dialogue with the British envoy and no reference was made to the council, whose attendant members were lectured equally with Betham on the responsibilities of Nepal's long friendship with Britain—'perpetual friendship', Sir Judha said, recalling the terms and the spirit of the treaty which ended the Nepal War. 'If you win, we will win with you. If you lose, we will lose with you.' For the second time in just over a quarter of a century Gurkhas had been committed to fight for the British Empire.

The Indian Army, other than its Gurkha regiments, had no option but to serve as the Viceroy and its commander-in-chief—which effectively meant Britain—ordered. Apart from its perennial North-West Frontier patrols which employed Gurkha battalions—a Gurkha did not have to cross the sea to get there—the Indian Army had also already demonstrated its superb professionalism in the Middle East. It fought there as a trained gap-filler just as it had done on the Western Front in the First World War before Britain could commit its new civilian armies and reinforcements from the then dominions of Canada, Australia and New Zealand. Now Britain, after the successful outcome of the aerial conflict with Germany in 1940, could count on supplementing its Indian divisions with a potential of more than forty Gurkha battalions.

Delay in Britain's formal approach to Nepal had deprived Gurkhas of the opportunity of taking part in the 4th Indian Division's contribution to General Wavell's North African victory over the Italians between December 1940 and February 1941; nor were they available to join the 4th and 5th Indian Divisions in ending the Italian occupation of Abyssinia and restoring Emperor Haile Selassie to his throne.

Other than on the North-West Frontier active service for Gurkhas in the Second World War began in Iraq, where it had ended for so many of them in the aftermath of 1914–18. Landing at Basra in April 1941, their presence in an army which was to become known as Paiforce, a Persia and Iraq force charged with safeguarding Britain's oil supplies and assisting the occupation of part of Persia, did not involve them in the miseries and hardships of their predecessors of the Mesopotamian campaign. Fortunately the Turks were not there to oppose them this second time round and lorries had relieved movement of some of its discomfort, the hard going straining the vehicles rather more than the passengers. There were compensations, too, the 2/3rd Gurkhas especially enjoying their football at Mosul; and there was plenty of game—duck, partridge and woodcock, and sumptuous feasts of wild boar. Perhaps the contrast with the conditions encountered by the 2/7th when they fought at Gurkha Mound and were besieged in Kut is best expressed by an allusion in the 3rd's regimental history to the men's enjoyment of a weekly steam bath, each village in northern Iraq having one such establishment.

Gurkha participation in Paiforce may appear trivial by comparison with previous performances, but it merits record if for no other reason than that it serves to reintroduce William Slim, the young subaltern of the Royal Warwickshire Regiment who had been so impressed by the bearing of the 1/6th Gurkhas at Gallipoli that he had joined the regiment. Ahead lay a partnership in which Major-General William Slim and the Gurkhas were to be crucially involved in saving India from the Japanese.

While the Gurkhas of Paiforce were enjoying their weekly Turkish baths the second battalions of the 1st, 2nd and 9th Gurkhas, brigaded as the 28th Brigade, were settling down at Ipoh and Taiping in central Malaya. So far, in fighting Britain's twentieth-century wars, the Nepalese hillmen had only sailed west. But now some of them, switched to their surprise, from an Iraq-bound convoy, had heaved gently east and into the Malacca Strait. On 3 September 1941, the second anniversary of the outbreak of the Second World War, they sailed in for a peaceful arrival at Port Swettenham. In Malaya as yet there was no war, and this was a blessing for which the commanders of the British, Indian and Australian forces were thankful as they trained and exercised their inadequately equipped men. When, in conjunction with the Japanese attack on Pearl Harbor on 7 December 1941, war came to Malaya, it was very soon over—though not before the three Gurkha battalions had fought with a resolution which elicited official Japanese recognition that, of all the nationalities opposed to them, the Gurkhas of Nepal were the most to be feared.

Unfortunately, Gurkha bravery and sacrifice was to prove of no avail. Command of the sea lost after the sinking of the battleship *Prince of Wales* and battle-cruiser *Repulse*, and without air support, the land defence of Malaya crumpled. With little to offer against tanks but rifle, bayonet and kukri the garrison troops were impotent in the face of a 750-mile Japanese advance down the Malayan peninsula to the causeway-connected island naval base of Singapore at its tip. On 14 February 1942 the Japanese accepted the surrender of Singapore and of 70,000 British, Australian, Indian and Gurkha troops.

The sense of humiliation experienced by Gurkhas and their British officers at a retreat which was beyond their physical or executive power to reverse could only be allayed by the determination of individuals and units to live up to regimental traditions—as with Rifleman Shiamlal Bura who had already been decorated in 1939 for bravery in Waziristan. Shiamlal, one forearm hit by Japanese machine-gun fire, asked a jemadar to cut it off so that he could carry on fighting. When, understandably, the officer declined, Shiamlal drew his kukri and severed it himself, plunging the stump into creosote from a latrine. Shiamlal survived a further fifteen days in the jungle before his wounds gave him no option but to surrender.

Other Gurkhas, fit enough to remain at large in the jungle, joined guerilla parties. Naik Narbahadur Thapa found to his astonishment that anti-Japanese activities were so well organised that he was expected to walk 5 miles a day through the jungle to attend lectures and conferences.

Gurkhas obey the last order, sometimes almost to a fault. As recently as the 1970s riflemen stationed at Church Crookham near Aldershot, Hampshire, who were detailed to sweep up and clear away all the autumnal leaves in the vicinity, did just that and, when they were finished, climbed the trees themselves to snip off the last offending leaves with scissors.

Naik Nakam Gurung's last order after escaping into the jungle when his battalion had been surrounded near Ipoh was to stay put at a remote spot. The trouble was that he had malaria and was considered unfit to continue with a party of fellow-escapers. Having been ordered by his subedar-major to remain where he was until the end of the war, this was precisely what Naik Nakam did. He built a shack, planted crops, trapped pig and caught fish in a nearby stream. The naik was still there on 20 October 1949 when, almost four years after the end of the war, a patrol of the 1/10th Gurkhas came across him. Returned to his unit, Nakam was congratulated on his good discipline, promoted and granted back-pay for his years as a jungle Robinson Crusoe.

Many of Nakam's comrades who were still fighting in Singapore when they received orders to cease fire were less fortunate. To them, condemned as they were to more than three years of hunger, torture and sickness in Japanese camps or on the Burma railway, the command to lay down their arms seemed even more unbelievable in retrospect than it had appeared at the time—especially to members of the 2/2nd Gurkhas. As news of the capitulation reached them they were actually advancing. . . .

To the north, pushing through Burma early in this disaster year of 1942, the Japanese very nearly penetrated India. There was little but great distances, mountains, hills, rivers and their ever-lengthening lines of communication to stop them. As it transpired, in May 1942 they over-reached themselves, and a combination of topography, the torrential rains of a Burma monsoon season, and to some extent the efforts of six battalions of Gurkhas—among other units—saved India and prevented the possibility of the Japanese shaking hands with their German allies somewhere between Delhi and Cairo. General Sir William Slim was to describe the end of the 900-mile retreat in these words: 'Soaked to the skin, rotten with fever . . . the rearguard marched into India . . . British, Indian and Gurkha, gaunt and ragged as scarecrows but they looked like soldiers too.'

Lieutenant-General Sir Francis Tuker in his post-war assessment of the retreat,* had a special word for the Gurkhas:

> With many who fought through those sad days, there remains one heartening memory—the cohesion and discipline of these Gurkha battalions and the astonishing manner in which their men, cut off in the forests, often wounded, always nearly famished, betrayed by the Burmese to their enemy, yet managed somehow to get back to their regiments, sometimes months later, carrying their arms and equipment and eager, despite their emaciated and lowered condition, to go into battle once more.

There was never any doubt in Slim's mind but that the Japanese would be thrown back whence they came, and now, west of the monsoon curtain, arduous training took place to achieve this object. The Japanese, using jungle paths, marching light, feeding frugally, hooking round and cutting off British formations, had employed methods and tactics which would suit Gurkhas, were they given the chance to reverse the role.

The retreat had ended along a line on the India-Burma borders which ran through Imphal and Kohima in the state of Manipur. It was an ideal area for Gurkha training, having regimental associations returning to the trouble with the Senapati at Imphal towards the end of the nineteenth century. Here in the hills Gurkha was paired with Gurkha, the couples not being allowed apart for twenty-four hours at a time, an essential ingredient of training to defeat the Japanese in the jungle. Fitness became a fetish. For instance, British officers of the 1/3rd were required to walk 6 miles into Kohima for a day's training and 6 miles back to their quarters each evening. There were long cross-

* *Gorkha: The Story of the Gurkhas of Nepal* (Constable, 1957).

country schemes over hills and through jungle for Gurkha companies, and there were military exercises, updated of course, but reminiscent of Roberts's exercise camps of another era. Intelligence ruses were also encouraged and the 1/3rd was rather pleased with itself for infiltrating four riflemen disguised as orange-selling Naga women into the 2/10th's mess at lunch-time, thus scoring the sub-machine-gun killing on paper of every officer in the battalion.

In North Africa in the spring and summer months of 1942 there was no monsoon to rain down a curtain between an army of retreat and its advancing opponents. Rommel's armoured division from Germany had put backbone into the effort of the German-Italian Axis troops, and reduced air support, occasioned by the needs of Greece, had made British use of the Libyan port of Benghazi impossible. Consequently, British forces had fallen back 200 miles east to Tobruk where, in the pendulum fighting of the desert war there took place on 21 June 1942 a British surrender followed by further retreat towards Egypt.

Here again, as at Singapore, Gurkhas found themselves in a surrender situation which did not accord with their aggressive, battle-winning instincts. Despite the gravity of their position individuals and units managed to extract a characteristic element of triumph from a disaster which was not of their making.

At Singapore Gurkhas would have fought, given the opportunity. At Tobruk a breakdown of communications offered such a chance and Subedar Bulbir Rai's platoon of the 2/7th continued to engage the enemy so successfully that it not only repulsed attacks on its position, but prevented two ships coming alongside and landing reinforcements. It was an action in the spirit of the same battalion's magnificent performance almost twenty-seven years before at Gurkha Mound in Mesopotamia. Not until twenty-four hours after the official surrender did the subedar accept defeat, and that was only when his water and ammunition were expended.

At Tobruk also there were moments when panic prevailed among some troops other than Gurkhas, and demoralised men passed through positions held by the 2/7th to comparative safety even as the Gurkhas stood their ground and fought. The examples set by Subedar-Major Sherbahadur Limbu and Subedar Jarasindu Lama of the 2/7th were especially inspiring. Responsible for a section of the port's 35-mile perimeter the 2/7th was cut off after German troops had entered the harbour area. Confronted by tanks and armoured cars the Gurkha officers assembled a freshly arrived and curious weapon known as a spigot mortar straight from its packing-case. Neither had fired or even handled the weapon before and the two men were astonished when, having aimed and fired the canister in the general direction of the enemy armour, the bomb, after striking the ground, ran along explosively like an overgrown firework until, finally, it blew up with a tremendous bang. This was not the weapon's designed behaviour but it had a salutary effect on the enemy.

Out of ammunition, confronted by increasing numbers of tanks, survivors of the 2/7th, as at Kut after Gurkha Mound, were obliged to join in the general surrender and make escape the next goal. Some had to bide their time, Subedar Bulbir Rai not getting away until he reached Italy as a prisoner of war; and Havildar Harkabahadur Rai, after being in Germany, escaped in the south of France and joined Free French parties operating along the Swiss borders. Others, immediately rejecting the humiliation of captivity, took to the desert to perish or, as with a few, to reach friendly lines. One havildar stumbled across the desert with three riflemen for thirty-six days before finding a British unit. Another, herded into a prisoner-of-war compound near Tobruk, bound his feet with cotton strips and stole away in the night as silently and effectively as the riflemen of the 1/5th who, with muffled boots, had evacuated Gallipoli under the noses of the Turks in the First World War.

In Burma early in 1943 after it had stopped raining there emerged to confront the Japanese an unorthodox British major-general who combined the qualities of the terrible Lony Ochter of the Nepal War and Lawrence of Arabia. Orde Wingate was already a guerilla specialist with experience in Palestine and Abyssinia when the 77th Indian Infantry Brigade was created to operate behind the Japanese lines on the far side of the Chindwin River. From the outset Wingate recognised Gurkhas as ideal material for this purpose, and so it came about that the 3/2nd joined the brigade, whose men were soon generally known as the Chindits.

Wingate's early operations were to be much criticised, General Tuker later commenting in his book *Gorkha* that 'a new Gurkha battalion was unlucky enough to accompany Wingate on his first operation in 1943'. Tuker condemned Wingate for intermingling Gurkhas with British soldiers and using Gurkhas as mule drivers, describing the mule as 'an animal to which the young wartime Gurkha was little accustomed and, in any case, a noisy and vulnerable means of transport such as no experienced commander would ever have borne with for one minute in such operations in such country'. Deploring heavy Gurkha losses under Wingate, Tuker summed up the expedition as 'clumsy'–'while the lessons, if any, that it taught were mainly what never to do again'. In making these strictures Tuker was justified, but there was another aspect. In the Far East as in Europe, and as in the Middle East in 1942, British military experience had been that of almost continuous retreat. For all the mistakes, Wingate's Chindits carried the war deep into Japanese-occupied territory and, so far as Gurkhas were concerned, confirmed that they were superior jungle fighters to the Japanese, whose easy conquests in Malaya and Burma had overblown their reputation in this role.

During 1943 Gurkhas were also involved elsewhere in Burma. They took part in an abortive attempt to return to the port of Rangoon by way of the Arakan on the east coast of the Bay of Bengal, and in fending off Japanese probes in the Imphal area near the Indian border where, in 1942, the Japanese advance had ended. While the Arakan effort failed, it enhanced the reputation of Gurkhas in that, ignoring monsoon conditions, they obtained several successes by rushing Japanese positions while the enemy sheltered from the downpour.

It was south of Imphal in the Tiddim area that the chief evidence first emerged of the value of jungle training. Here in a battle for a feature known as Basha Hill, the 1/4th and 2/5th justified all the endeavour that the riflemen and their officers had put into preparing to avenge the previous year's retreat.

'*Ayo Gurkhali!*'—Here come the Gurkhas! This is the battle-cry of Gurkhas when their blood is up. If the Japanese had not heard it hitherto they would not mistake it after young Havildar Gaje Gale's charge at Basha Hill. To the Japanese it seemed unbelievable that an enemy, after being mortared, then facing close-range machine-gun fire and lobbed hand-grenades in a less than 20-foot wide approach, could still press on. Yet Havildar Gaje's teenage platoon kept going until it was in the midst of the enemy, and then the riflemen went to work with their kukris until the Japanese turned and fled from the hill-crest. Standing victorious on the summit the havildar, soaked in blood and wounded all over his body by grenade splinters, refused

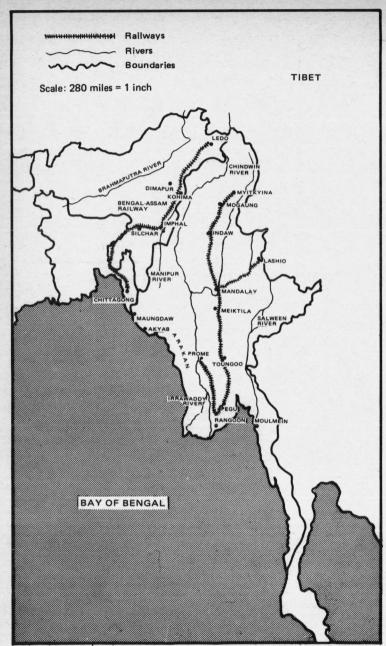

Figure 3   Burma

to have his multiple wounds dressed and continued to refuse medical aid until ordered to receive it by a British officer. He was awarded the Victoria Cross.

For all the hardships endured by Gurkhas in encounters with Japanese troops along the India-Burma borders another year would pass before the cry '*Ayo Gurkhali!*' was to herald the great drive of Slim's Fourteenth Army, the 'Forgotten Army', to destroy the Japanese divisions in Burma.

In North Africa in this same year, 1943, Gurkhas were vitally involved in the offensive which defeated Rommel's Afrika Korps and resulted in the linking up in Tunisia of westward-pushing British forces and eastward-advancing United States troops. Indeed, had Gurkhas made no further contribution to the allied victory in North Africa their presence would have been amply rewarded by their conduct in a series of actions which followed their appearance in General Montgomery's set-piece battle at Alamein.

In mid-March 1943 the Eighth Army had advanced through Libya and pushed into Tunisia where further progress was impeded by the Mareth Line, a 20-mile-long defence system running from the coast to the natural barrier of the Matmata Hills. Although a successful long-range flanking movement was carried out, reduction of this line and freedom to proceed towards Tunis called for the knocking out of a Matmata position from which enemy artillery was shelling an important road junction. To enter the hills and silence the guns was a task tailor-made for Gurkhas, and the 1/2nd of General Tuker's 'Red Eagles', the 4th Indian Division, made a forced march from Tripoli to undertake it. Two Gurkha platoons climbed to the vicinity of the offending guns—and they were very soon out of action.

'*Ayo Gurkhali!*' The war-cry had frozen the Japanese with fear across the world at Basha Hill and now it terrified the Germans in Tunisia. Head-on the Gurkhas charged, kukris held high, and into a hail of machine-gun fire until the momentum of their attack had carried them into the midst of the enemy. The Germans fought courageously, but within minutes enough was enough and the survivors fled, their screams echoing in the hills. After the Gurkhas had wiped their kukris and returned them to their scabbards they counted 15 enemy dead. Most of the bodies were headless. The two Gurkha platoons had lost 4 riflemen.

Two weeks later, as Rommel attempted to hold a new position 20 miles north of the now invested Mareth Line, the Gurkhas were presented with another situation, to meet the demands of which they were ideally suited by an accumulation of more than a hundred years of Indian frontier experience. Winston Churchill, writing as British Prime Minister, explained the problem in a letter of 3 May 1943 to Marshal Stalin in Moscow: 'The peculiar mountainous character of the country, with flat plains commanded by rugged, upstanding peaks, each of which is a fortress, aids the enemy's defence and slows up our advance. I hope however to have good news for you before the end of this month.'*

The good news reached Stalin sooner than Churchill had expected. On 13 May, General Sir Harold Alexander, Middle East Commander-in-Chief, signalled the Prime Minister: 'It is my duty to report that the Tunisian campaign is over. All enemy resistance has ceased. We are masters of the North African shores.'

It was a victory on a large scale to which Gurkhas had contributed in part and in which their achievement in one important action was out of all proportion to the numbers involved.

* *The Second World War*, Vol. IV (Cassell, 1951).

To speed up the advance through the 'peculiar mountainous country' it would be necessary to take a high point called Fatnassa, but the staff had ruled out such a move as being altogether too difficult in favour of a straightforward coastal assault. There was, however, one field commander who disagreed. General Tuker, commanding the 4th Indian Division, knew his Gurkhas. He had campaigned with them on the North-West Frontier in Waziristan and he proposed that Gurkhas should climb the heights, make a night attack and achieve what colleagues lacking Indian Army experience regarded as the impossible. After his plan had been accepted even Tuker held inner doubts as to whether he had allowed himself to be over-persuaded as a former Gurkha regimental officer by his knowledge of and admiration for the Nepalese hillmen. Certainly, with its precipitous approaches, its deep chimneys, its escarpments and high, forbidding pinnacles, Fatnassa, defended by a mixed force of Italians and Germans, appeared formidable in the extreme.

Under an early evening moon, crescented as it happened almost to the shape of the blade of a kukri, riflemen of the 1/2nd Gurkhas moved quietly forward. Half an hour before midnight the leading sections started their climb. Up they went, silently groping their way in a rocky chimney, silently until the peace of the desert night was broken by a scream as an enemy look-out was chopped to the ground by the blow of a kukri. Fierce hand-to-hand fighting ensued.

At one point an anti-tank gun obstructed a narrow path, but a party of riflemen rushed the gun, much as their predecessors had rushed the Afridis from the goat-track on the hill at Dargai, and Havildar Bibahadur Pun personally accounted for three of the enemy with his kukri and wounded several others. Elsewhere, another narrow and very steep path led to a commanding crest occupied by Italian troops. To reach it involved crossing open ground swept by machine-gun fire and erupting with grenade explosions. Through this inferno hurtled Subedar Lalbahadur Thapa, cutting down several of the enemy with his kukri as he went, and shooting others with his pistol. Followed by several riflemen he charged a machine-gun covering the path, disposing of two of its crew of four with kukri cuts while his comrades shot the others.

Tuker's main attack was not due to follow up until the early hours of the morning, but the enemy had had enough, some jumping off high cliffs to their deaths in sheer terror. The 1/2nd and 1/9th Gurkhas had cleared the heights and the Eighth Army would shortly be able to continue its advance—but not immediately, because the initial advantage was thrown away by the inability of tanks to be in the right place at the right time. Gurkhas, however, had become accustomed to seeing opportunities created by their expertise and valour thrown away. On a smaller scale this disappointment resembled the shambles at Sari Bair in Gallipoli. In retrospect Subedar Lalbahadur's Victoria Cross provided some compensation.

Gurkhas were to feature in one further demonstration of their distinctive frontier-type qualities before the end came for the Axis in North Africa. After the Mareth Line had been breached and beyond the scene of Fatnassa, the Eighth Army's need to break through the next German defensive line around Enfidaville called for the reduction of a position at Djebel Garci, another peak fastness of the type and character of which Winston Churchill had informed Joseph Stalin.

It would be unjust to the many other fine regiments of the Indian Army were this account of the Gurkhas not to acknowledge the overall merit of its non-Gurkha regiments, and in this instance the particular steadfastness of the 4/6th Rajputana Rifles, a battalion drawn from a martial people among whom well-born Nepalese traditionally sought their wives. At Djebel Garci on a mid-April day in' 1943 the Rajputanas went in first, suffering grievously in an action which developed into one of the hardest fought hand-to-hand encounters of the Second World War. Every British officer had fallen, as also had Havildar-Major Chelu Ram who was awarded a posthumous Victoria Cross for rallying the leaderless riflemen at the time the 1/9th Gurkhas charged.

There followed a kukri bloodbath, Havildar-Major Dhirbahadur slaughtering four Germans as though they were goats for the pot and Rifleman Nirbahadur Mal disappearing into a milling mass of flailing arms and fists to reappear surrounded by twelve German bodies as the remainder of the enemy took to their heels. When the Germans had departed forty-four dead were counted.

But Gurkha business at Djebel Garci was not yet concluded, because the enemy had fled uphill to fresh defensive positions. Now, in the tradition of the men of the 3rd and 5th Gurkhas who had pioneered the art of scouting in the Tirah campaign of 1897–8, Jemadar Dewan Singh Basnet reconnoitred ahead. . . . Halt! The jemadar responded to a challenge by creeping forward to take a look at his challenger. He had not understood the tongue and he wished to confirm that it was a foe. He closed on the sentry and recognised the shape of a German helmet. In moments head and helmet were on the ground. 'He was fumbling with his weapon so I cut off his head with my kukri,' the jemadar reported. He decapitated three more Germans, but a fourth, whom he had only wounded, cried out, his screams alerting the remainder of the enemy force. Surrounded, the jemadar fought until his kukri was seized in the mêlée. Fortunately for the Gurkha his opponent, unfamiliar with such a weapon, failed to strike him down. Nevertheless, he was beaten to the ground where he pretended to lie dead—and certainly there was enough blood on his face to help him feign death convincingly.

After a while the jemadar wiped the blood out of his eyes and looked about him—and there close at hand and unattended was a German machine-gun. His thoughts now turned to reaching the gun and 'killing the lot'. To the Gurkha's dismay, approaching daylight and the arrival of his own platoon hurling grenades robbed him of his ambition. Reunited with his men and deprived of his kukri the jemadar, too cut about to draw his pistol for himself, asked a rifleman to place it in his hand and then resumed command of the platoon.

Shortly afterwards the 1/9th, almost as if it were old times on the frontier, were relieved by those great friends of Gurkha regiments, the Gordon Highlanders, the battalion marching off with the following tribute from General Tuker in its colonel's pocket: 'The more I hear of your fine battalion and its fight on Garci hills the more certain I am that it has written one of the most glorious pages in its history.'

The North African struggle over, Gurkhas moved on to Italy where the allied invasion and campaign provided opportunities for many more such pages to be written.

CHAPTER NINE

The Road to Rome

In Italy the road to Rome was the road towards victory, but in early 1944 the allied northward advance to the city was brought to an abrupt halt by the spirited German defence of the fortified Benedictine monastery sitting atop the forbidding heights of Monte Cassino. Had the American landings at Anzio, to the north beyond Cassino, been immediately successful, then the mountain position might have been turned. However, an Anzio setback and the failure early in January of an American attempt to carry Cassino in one storming assault had stopped the march on Rome.

A highly determined German occupying force, which included paratroops of the élite 1st Parachute Division, had settled into a ready-made defensive position and was intent upon staying there and controlling the only route to the north through the mountains that straddled the narrowest part of Italy between the Tyrrhenian and Adriatic Seas. At this stage, Gurkhas of General Tuker's 4th Indian Division, which was part of General Alexander's Eighth Army from North Africa, arrived. In their first efforts the Gurkhas came so close to taking German positions around the monastery walls that, as at Sari Bair in the Gallipoli campaign, seizure of the key to an overwhelming success was momentarily within their grasp.

However, after suffering heavy casualties the riflemen of the 1/2nd and 1/9th had to be withdrawn, as were those of the 2/7th who, while detailed to act as porters for the assault, had been obliged to unburden themselves, draw kukris and fight.

For several weeks little more than skirmishing took place and then in mid-March a fresh assault, mounted by the New Zealand Corps and Indian Division, involved the Gurkhas in an exceptionally daring manoeuvre. The aim was to move the 1/9th under cover of darkness and through drenching rain to a rocky position named Hangman's Hill within about 100 yards of one corner of the monastery. As daylight came, and it seemed from a distance that, in view of fierce fighting during the attempt it had failed, the New Zealand artillery opened fire on Hangman's Hill. Then, sharply the order to cease fire was given. Incredibly, one company of Gurkhas had reported in a scarcely audible radio message that it had occupied the position just below the monastery garden. Back up the mountainside to a wounded officer, Captain Drinkall, and his company of the 1/9th crackled this order: 'Hold on at all costs'.

Now, Lieutenant-Colonel Nangle of the 1/9th ordered the remainder of the battalion to join their comrades at Hangman's Hill. Conveniently, there was a goat-track winding steeply up a ravine. Up and up went the Gurkhas until, just as they glimpsed their objective above them, they came under heavy bombardment. There was no advantage in waiting and, leading a company of riflemen, Captain Samuels hurled himself into the Hangman's Hill position. He was just in time to help prevent the remnants of the defenders from being overrun. Seizing a Bren gun from a dead Gurkha he fought off an attack by German paratroops at almost point-blank range. Colonel Nangle arrived with the rest of his men and for two weeks the 1/9th fought off attempt after attempt to dislodge them from their precarious perch beneath the very walls of the monastery.

As the days passed the Gurkhas went on reduced rations, and supplies dropped from the air tended to bounce away out of reach. Eventually, there was no option but to withdraw. Of the battalion-strong 1/9th that went up the mountain only 177 Gurkhas came down. On a rock at Hangman's Hill there is now displayed the crossed kukris emblem of the 9th Gurkhas, commemorating in perpetuity, to quote the definitive undertaking of Nepal's treaty with Britain, the valour of the regiment's 1st Battalion.

On the morning of 18 May Cassino was at last captured, and the Free Poles ran up their red-and-white flag over the shattered monastery. After this allied victory, Gurkhas of the 1/5th, 2/7th and 1/9th were all heavily involved in the general advance which carried the Allies beyond Rome and up against the Gothic Line, the 2/3rd and 2/4th joining up with them from the Adriatic coast in June.

At the beginning of August three fresh Gurkha battalions, the 2/6th, 2/8th and 2/10th were landed at Taranto. From the outset there was something very different about these battalions. They had Dodge trucks to carry them north to the front and they represented a departure from Gurkha practice. As the 43rd Gurkha Lorried Brigade they were not necessarily expected to march. Yet lorries cannot of themselves overcome hilly country and stubbornly defended ridges and in early September the three battalions. were engaged in their habitual role of forcing the enemy out of naturally defensible positions along the Adriatic seaboard.

Desperately resisting advancing armies on the Western Front, on the Eastern Front and in Italy, German opposition encountered by the Gurkhas in the north of Italy was among the stiffest they were to experience in the Second World War. As was to be expected in these circumstances no quarter was given or expected and there were ferocious encounters from which both Gurkha and German emerged with credit. In the battle for Sant'Arcangelo, north-west of San Marino, a company of the 2/10th, unsupported by tanks and lacking anti-tank weapons, was confronted by enemy tanks and infantry in a strong counter-attack. There was nothing the riflemen could do to defend themselves against such odds. Courageously they climbed out of their inadequate emergency trenches and interrupted the enemy's advance with a desperate charge, intent upon fighting until the inevitable end. Among the Gurkhas who died this late September day was Rifleman Ganjabahadur Rai. Face to face with a very large German who towered over his small frame, Ganjabahadur duelled, kukri to rifle-butt, until the German could parry the blows no longer and was chopped to the ground. The Gurkha had severely wounded another of the enemy when he was shot down. After the engagement the 2/10th took possession of the rifle with which Ganjabahadur had duelled. Dented as it was by kukri cuts it became a prized trophy of the battalion.

Some VCs do not survive to receive the supreme award for valour and among the ten Victoria Crosses won by Gurkhas in the Second World War two were awarded posthumously towards the end of the campaign in Italy.

Outside San Marino in September 1944 the 1/9th, a battalion which by this stage of the campaign had probably contributed quite enough pages of glory to its regiment's history, was held up by a strongly defended bend in the main road leading towards the city. Inevitably, a German machine-gun was the chief obstacle, but Rifleman Sherbahadur Thapa and a companion charged it, killing the German gunner and putting his comrades to flight. However, the machine-gun nest had hardly been evacuated when the enemy returned in greater numbers, wounding Sherbahadur's fellow-countryman. In a swift and agile response the Gurkha rifleman, firing his Bren gun from the hip, drove back the counter-attack and, astonishingly, put several more machine-guns out of action. For two hours the rifleman stood in an exposed position, refusing orders to withdraw, yet covering the withdrawal of his comrades until he was out of ammunition. By this time an exasperated British major of the 1/9th, to whose orders Sherbahadur had turned a deaf ear, shouted across the Italian country-side that he rather thought that the rifleman had done enough for one day. Sherbahadur was not of the same opinion. Although under continuous fire he attempted to rescue two fellow-riflemen who lay wounded under the very noses of the Germans. After Sherbahadur had brought one back it seemed that his life must be charmed. He was returning with the second man when the major dashed into the open to give a hand. In that moment three gallant members of the 1/9th Gurkhas were killed.

11 November 1944 was the anniversary of the 1914-18 war armistice, as good a day as any for the 1/5th Gurkhas to find themselves ordered to take on the 'impossible'; which generals considered just possible if Gurkhas were involved. Monte San Bartolo stood atop a high bluff remi-niscent of the hill that was renamed Gurkha Bluff on the Gallipoli peninsula. It was situated in open hill country. There were steep approaches and any soldier attempting to scale them could expect to die in a hail of covering machine-gun fire. In the tradition handed down from Dargai Hill, a platoon which had been detailed to recon-noitre the area sent forward two scouts. Reaching the bottom of the bluff unnoticed Rifleman Thaman Gurung and his fellow-Gurkha began to clutch their way up the open face when they saw the helmets of two Germans in a trench just below the summit. The enemy had not seen the two scouts and were in the act of training a machine-gun on a larger party of Gurkhas following up when Thaman, materialising almost as if he were a genie, secured the immediate surrender of the astonished machine-gun crew.

Leaving his fellow-scout to guard the prisoners, Rifle-man Thaman saw that the follow-up party was again endangered, this time by several German soldiers who were on the point of rolling hand-grenades down the cliff-face and into their midst as though taking aim in a bowling-alley. Regardless of being exposed to fire from another machine-gun, Thaman went forward, his sub-machine-gun blazing, enabling the follow-up party to reach the bluff.

As the platoon assembled it became the target of a tremendous burst of machine-gun fire from Monte San Bartolo itself and from either side. There was no option but to withdraw and in this moment Thaman leaped up, firing until he was out of ammunition and then hurling two hand-grenades of his own and two others he had found. If this were not enough for one man, he snatched a Bren gun from another member of the platoon and rushed to the top of the bluff again. There, the Bren at his hip, he let loose at the enemy like a man possessed, a dark silhouette standing out almost three-dimensionally against the blue of the Italian sky.

Rifleman Thaman had won time for his comrades to reach safety. Almost out of ammunition he was on the point of attempting to rejoin them when the silhouette crumpled and another posthumous Victoria Cross was added to the Gurkha roll of honour.

CHAPTER TEN

The Chink in Slim's Armour

Across the world from Hangman's Hill in early 1944 the Japanese announced their 'March on Delhi'. General Slim, commander of the British Fourteenth Army, had anticipated the drive for India which he had known must come by preparing his own offensive. First, however, he decided to withdraw in the face of the enemy's main attack on the Imphal plain with a view to launching his counter-offensive after the Japanese had expended themselves and extended their lines of communication. Withdrawal, though, did not mean that the Japanese were not to be molested. The longer their lines of supply became, the more vulnerable would they be to cuts, and this is where Wingate's Chindits, and notably their Gurkha element, re-enter the scene.

With the objects of dislocating the Japanese Army's supply railway running north from Rangoon harbour, of helping the US-Chinese force in the north, including Merrill's Marauders, and of opening a route to China, one Chindit brigade, the 16th British, marched 450 miles over mountains and through jungle southward from Ledo to an area where the railway passed through Indaw. Just as ambitiously, considering the jungle terrain, between 6 and 11 March 7,500 men, mules and baggage of the 77th and 111th Infantry Brigades of British and Gurkha troops were flown in, at first by gliders to prepare air-strips, and then by transport aircraft which flew in on the freshly made landing-grounds 100 miles inside Japanese-held territory.

The Gurkha was nature's Chindit. A born hunter, his jungle craft was an incalculable asset to his British officers. Blending into the jungle's light and shade, silently observant, listening and melting into the foliage whence he came, to report on enemy strength and dispositions, he scouted time and time again to within yards of an unaware enemy. It never ceased to amaze the British soldiers who served with them in the Chindits that Gurkhas carried out such missions with that same sense of discipline and pride in getting things right that inspired a battalion to dismantle and pitch again an entire tented camp—as the Royal Marines observed in the Arakan—because the pegs were out of line! It was hardly surprising that Slim, a soldier's general, and looking every inch of it with his jutting jaw and firm mouth, placed so much reliance on his beloved Gurkhas and their British officers. Brigadier Michael Calvert, the Chindit leader of the 77th Brigade, was to describe this infatuation as 'the chink in Slim's armour', writing: 'He could never rid himself of his soft spot for the Gurkhas. . . . He could never be too hard on his fellow-Gurkha generals [British officers promoted from Gurkha regiments] and treated them with a leniency he did not accord to others. He knew that the Gurkhas were, in spite of their badinage, his most faithful and reliant supporters both in Fourteenth Army and in GHQ India and he could always turn to them when the going was rough.'*

In Burma in 1944 the going was exceedingly rough for Calvert—affectionately known as 'mad Mike' because of his personal exploits. Since the air landings of March Calvert's brigade had fought its way more than 150 miles north from the Indaw area with the aim of taking Mogaung on the railway, an effort which had cost the 3rd Battalion of Slim's old

* *Slim* (Pan/Ballantine, 1973).

regiment, the 6th Gurkhas, nearly 500 casualties. Where earlier Chinese troops from the north had failed to move on Mogaung, Calvert's force, depleted and debilitated by three months of jungle living conditions and warfare, succeeded, winning three Victoria Crosses in the process— the Chinese reappearing to claim some of the credit.

Among these Mogaung gallantry awards was the Victoria Cross won by Captain M. Allmand of the 3/6th Gurkhas. His decoration resulted from a remarkable performance with a kukri, all the more so for a British officer who could not be expected to be as adept with the curved knife as were those for whom it was a natural weapon. Held up by the stubborn defence of a bridge, and after thirty Gurkhas had died in attempting to take it, Allmand rushed the Japanese on his own, throwing hand-grenades and hacking the enemy down with his kukri as he went. The next day Allmand, leading the attack, took another well-defended position in the face of heavy machine-gun fire. In yet another assault during which he showed no regard whatsoever for his personal safety Allmand, limping heavily with trench foot, was hit. His award was post-humous.

Major F. G. Blaker's battalion, the 3/9th, was involved together with the 3/4th in a typical Gurkha undertaking: a hill commanding part of the railway-line needed to be cleared of Japanese machine-gun nests. Blaker's company had advanced to the point when it encountered the classic situation which had confronted Gurkhas in many places in two world wars, a crest that to be taken must be assaulted under almost point-blank machine-gun fire. Blaker led his men forward and kept on going, although wounded by a grenade burst. When the major reached the Japanese machine-guns he charged. Several bullets passed through Blaker's body but he shouted his men on until they had cleared the crest. They were carrying him down the hill when he died.

The other Victoria Cross hero of Calvert's brigade at Mogaung was Rifleman Tulbahadur Pun who, disdaining danger in almost identical fashion to Rifleman Thaman at Monte San Bartolo, swung a Bren gun from his hip and charged a defended house across open ground, his stocky shape silhouetted by the early morning light. Whether or not the Japanese gunners were distracted by the sheer bravado of his action, Tulbahadur survived and captured two machine-guns which had been pouring fire at him.

While the Chindits harassed Japanese communications, Slim's troops continued to fall back before the much-trumpeted March on Delhi. Gurkhas of the 1/3rd, 1/4th, 2/5th, 1/7th and 1/10th of Major-General G. T. 'Punch' Cowan's 17th Indian Division—known as the 'Black Cats' because of their divisional emblem—would have preferred to have been going the other way, but here and there they satisfied their natural instincts by slowing down what had developed into a perilously rapid advance by the enemy. Nevertheless, the Japanese had soon crossed the Chindwin and pushed Fourteenth Army troops back to Imphal, which the 17th Division entered at the beginning of April. It was here that, after three weeks of fighting, Cowan told his Gurkhas and other troops what he knew they needed to hear: 'We are the better troops, and every man in this division knows it. The moment we have the Jap on the move, we've got him'.

Suddenly, it seemed that Slim's scheme for a planned withdrawal might have misfired, and Japanese propaganda announcements of a March on Delhi began to assume an air of reality as imperial troops looking down from the Somra Hills into Assam raised the flag of the Rising Sun on Indian soil. The Japanese swept round Imphal and encircled it while, to the north, reaching the pleasant hospital hill station of Kohima, gateway to a pass through the Assam Hills and the road to Delhi far beyond, they cut off its garrison from India and its source of resupply.

In these dangerous weeks of the first half of 1944 Gurkhas, as individuals and at all strengths, fought so many courageous actions that it would be invidious to select examples were not such descriptions illustrative of the whole. At all costs the Japanese had to be kept back from India, particularly from the all-important lifeline of the Bengal-Assam railway. Every man who fought at Imphal, Kohima (whose defenders included a Nepalese regiment from Katmandu) and in the Silchar Track and Tiddim Road areas, knew that upon his steadfastness depended the saving of India from the Japanese and their defector friends of the subversive Indian National Army. The need to control westward routes, the sole communication links for a modern army's mechanised units, was paramount, and when positions offering command of these routes fell into Japanese hands they had to be cleared. Such a hill position overlooked the Silchar Track, and forty riflemen of the 2/5th Gurkhas, under Subedar Netrabahadur Thapa, were given the task of ridding it of the enemy.

Placed on a nearby feature mapped as Mortar Bluff the subedar and his men were immediately subjected to a night of heavy rain and shellfire followed by an infantry attack. Very soon half the men in the subedar's force were casualties and the remainder were almost out of ammunition. The riflemen were young and not very experienced, though none the less brave for that, and the subedar encouraged them as they held off the Japanese. When it appeared that he was likely to be overwhelmed he calmly made a request on his field telephone for friendly artillery to put down a barrage on his own position. He also asked for some more ammunition and a supply of grenades. But the torrential rain of the night had made the approaches to Mortar Bluff very difficult to climb. As daylight came, the Japanese saw eight Gurkhas slipping and slithering on the muddy hillside as they struggled to carry up ammunition, and shot them down.

Ignoring the peril the subedar went down the hill to collect ammunition from the dead men. Surviving this, his kukri in one hand and hurling grenades with the other, he led a charge against the enemy. When his body was found the subedar was still gripping the kukri with which he had slain a Japanese who lay beside him. To Subedar Netrabahadur Thapa of the 2/5th went a posthumous Victoria Cross.

After Netrabahadur's death Havildar Lachimbahadur Thapa counted only five men of the original forty who were in a fit condition to carry on. The survivors had no alternative but to hump away as many of the wounded as they could manage.

Shortly afterwards two fresh companies of the 2/5th attempted to return to the top of Mortar Bluff. They had climbed to within 100 yards of the summit when machinegun fire and shells from a 37 mm concealed in the jungle stopped them. As on so many previous and similar occasions a Gurkha was ready to apply the only remedy. Leading a handful of riflemen, Naik Agansing Rai rushed the machine-gun and Mortar Bluff was in the 2/5th's possession again.

But now the heavier gun firing from the jungle made continued tenancy problematical and Agansing decided it would have to be silenced. Having led his small party into the open, Agansing tore across it and dived into the jungle with his men. When the Gurkhas reached the enemy position Agansing and three others killed the gun-crew of five Japanese and put the 37 mm out of action.

The loss and recovery of Mortar Bluff and the side incidents of these affairs had distracted the 2/5th from their prime objective—clearing of the Japanese-held position which dominated the Silchar Track. An assault was ordered from Mortar Bluff and Agansing was in the thick of it. As riflemen fell dead around him, victims of machine-gun bullets and exploding grenades which, incredibly, left the naik unscathed, Agansing, carrying a sub-machine-gun, closed right in on a bunker harbouring the machine-gun and four Japanese. The Gurkha killed them, and was subsequently awarded the Victoria Cross.

By such acts were Kohima and Imphal relieved, India saved and Slim enabled to play his touch-and-go waiting game until the March on Delhi stumbled to a halt on the Imphal plain and it was time at last for the Fourteenth Army to implement its commander's long-planned offensive and destroy the Japanese Army in Burma.

As the rainy season reached its heaviest point in June 1944, and the Japanese counted the cost of the March on Delhi—53,000 casualties out of 100,000 men—they hoped that the monsoon curtain which had protected their enemy two years earlier would now ring down the Burma act until they could recover and reorganise. But Slim was to give them no respite. His Fourteenth Army pursued them, harassed them eastward and southward, each adversary drenched by the monsoon rains and dragging his equipment through seas of mud and up down slippery hillsides, right back to the Chindwin River and down the road to Mandalay. Down in the Arakan, however, rain falling at the rate of 20 inches a week obstructed progress.

No Gurkha would wish history to deny full and glowing recognition of the contribution during the last phase in Burma of other regiments of the Indian Army, of British troops, nor indeed of the ever-increasing air support which became available during the closing stages of the war in Europe in early 1945. However, that said, this is an account of the Gurkhas at arms and, notwithstanding all their own efforts on land, sea and in the air, no Indian or British fellow-holder of the Burma Star, the medal of the campaign, would ever grudge the hillmen from Nepal their full due. Slim, comparing the Asian soldier with the British infantryman, generalised of the former that he was 'usually more careless of death, less encumbered by mental doubts or humanitarian sentiment, not so moved by slaughter and mutilation', and in saying this he was almost certainly thinking of the Asian fighting man he knew best—the Gurkha.

As the Fourteenth Army harried a ravaged, often starving and desperate Japanese Army in retreat, such attributes assisted a soldier in his task. Certainly they were needed as Gurkhas took the road to Mandalay in 1945. To the 4/10th early that year, Mandalay, lying enticingly across the Irrawaddy River and on the railway south to Rangoon, was prospectively as attractive a prize as Baghdad, the city of the *Arabian Nights*, had seemed to the 2nd Battalion of the same regiment in the Mesopotamian campaign of the First World War. The Japanese had staged a violent counter-attack north of the city as though somehow, considering the magic of Mandalay and its associations with Rudyard Kipling, its fall would spell the beginning of the end for them in Burma.

Possibly the most savage fighting in beating off the counter-attack took place after the 20th Indian Division had forced the Irrawaddy in February and established a bridgehead at Myinmu. South of the bridgehead lay the village of Talingon and here the 4/10th Gurkhas repulsed an assault by waves of Japanese troops who, bayonetting their way into their midst, fought to the death in a mêlée of individual kukri and bayonet duels. When either Gurkha or Japanese lost his weapon fists were used.

The Gurkha battalion had been helped by being forewarned that an attack was imminent. This forewarning came not through aerial reconnaissance but from the unsophisticated yet totally reliable agency of a pair of Gurkhas sited, all too conspicuously for their own comfort, in a tree overlooking a path up which at least some troops of any Japanese attack must pass. After telephoning news of the

Japanese advance as casually as a wholesale grocer's sales-man might call up his office with an order, Naik Dhanbahadur Limbu and Rifleman Karnabahadur Rai dropped three grenades on the Japanese commanding officer as he paused to confer with four officers directly below the tree. The Japanese were so bemused that they never discovered where the grenades had come from, and the two Gurkha observers stayed up the tree all night until the battle which ensued all around them was over. When they descended they sought field dressings for wounds which their own grenades had inflicted on their backsides.

Shortly, the 1st Devons moved in to relieve the 4/10th Gurkhas who had lost 50 men killed and 127 wounded. Finding more than 500 Japanese corpses they summoned two armoured bulldozers to deal with them. Subsequently, the Japanese admitted that they had lost nearly 1,000 men in the battle.

In early March Slim's troops reached Mandalay, and there they caught their breath as they saw shining in the sun before them a multitude of pagodas and monasteries covering Mandalay Hill. The 4/10th Gurkhas made a night attack and, ordered to carry the holy hill, fought their way up to the temple, which they entered at dawn. This was no place for small-arms' fire and in any event the Gurkhas were always more confident in the kukri when fighting at close range. In a ferocious bloodletting the Gurkhas chased the terrified Japanese in and out of the temple aisles and pillars until the enemy were either headless or screaming in headlong flight. Very soon, astonished British troops heard the pealing of temple bells. The Gurkhas had found the bell-ropes.

There followed a race to reach Rangoon before May and the onset of the next monsoon. Gurkhas were everywhere in this dash and particularly prominent were the 1/3rd, 1/7th and the 1/10th. Lieutenant-Colonel John Masters of the 4th Gurkhas and commander of the Chindits of 111th

Indian Infantry Brigade, observed the start of the push. Masters, who was to become known after the war as a novelist and the author among other books of *Bowhani Junction*, has added his footnote to Slim's comparison of Gurkhas and British troops. Describing the departure of a convoy of vehicles as it crashed past Slim and his assembled generals, Masters wrote of how the British soldiers cheered and yelled while the Gurkhas, as imperturbable as ever, 'went by sitting stiffly to attention, whole truckloads bouncing four feet in the air without change of expression'.* This, Masters summed up, was the old Indian Army going down to the attack for the last time, exactly 250 years after the Honourable East India Company had enlisted its first ten sepoys on the Coromandel coast.

Since the port of Rangoon would now be essential for the supply of Slim's army an amphibious force was despatched to seize it. The landing was unopposed. The Japanese had left and withdrawn to Pegu in the direction of the advancing Gurkhas and the remainder of the Fourteenth Army.

On 3 May 1945 Rangoon fell—and so did the rain.

---

* *The Road Past Mandalay* (Michael Joseph, 1961).

CHAPTER ELEVEN

Bravest of the Brave

The next stops were Malaya, Singapore, Thailand, Java, Hong Kong and Japan. Atom bombs on Hiroshima and Nagasaki enforced Japanese capitulation on 14 August 1945, thus preventing the anticipated opposed landings and more bitter fighting for each of these places and all the way to Tokyo.

Gurkha battalions which had been prepared to carry the war back to Malaya where Gurkhas had suffered so badly in the New Year retreat of 1942 now went ashore to round up Japanese prisoners and welcome their own comrades on their release. Fighting in Malaya, the Middle East, Italy and Burma ten Gurkha regiments had lost 10,000 dead, with 15,000 wounded or taken prisoner, out of the 100,000 men who had come down from the hills of Nepal to fight alongside British soldiers. Yet if there had been sufficient war and fighting in this period to satisfy the most martial of their number, there were those whose eyes misted over and reddened with fury—as is customary with Gurkhas when they are very angry—when they learned of the prisoner-of-war experiences of their captured fellow-riflemen.

After the fall of Singapore the Japanese had instituted a deliberate policy of ill-treatment of Gurkhas, having failed to win converts with an immediate pat-on-the shoulder, you're-an-Asian-and-one-of-us effort to persuade them to join the Indian National Army. Whereas numbers of Indian troops had signed for the INA, hardly a Gurkha was coerced—and most of the exceptions were wily riflemen who seized the opportunity to be marched off to Burma where they escaped into the jungle, some to rejoin their regiments, others to perish in the attempt. Enfuriated by their failure to recruit men whom they knew to be excellent soldiers, the Japanese reserved the most barbaric measures for the Gurkha officers who, by their example, continued to inspire the other ranks not to succumb to enemy blandishments after the British officers had been removed. A favourite Japanese pastime was to imprison the hillmen in iron cages, as happened to Subedar-Major Chethabahadur of the 2/9th, who thereupon advised his guards to kill him and save everybody's time.

Gradually it dawned on the Japanese that perhaps, after all, there was something in the regular Gurkha remonstration that they could not volunteer for the Indian National Army because they were not Indians and came from the independent state of Nepal which enjoyed a treaty of friendship in perpetuity with Britain. Lodging a group of Gurkha officers in a comfortable bungalow in Penang they offered them positions in the Japanese Army. The Gurkhas demurred and were returned to the discomforts of the camps.

Gurkhas as prisoners of war may have been deprived of their kukris but in their spirit and bearing they possessed a moral weapon which no captor could remove from them. In the First World War the Turks, impressed by Gurkha prison camp discipline, had improved the lot of their captives. Similarly, in south-east Asia as the months passed the Japanese began visibly to respect Gurkha prisoners, at times to the point of ill-concealed admiration. That the Japanese had managed to induce Indians rather than Gurkhas to join the Indian National Army should not be

taken to infer that every Indian Army prisoner was eager
to defect. Individual Indians, particularly officers, were as
courageous as Gurkhas in defiance of their captors. Indeed,
Gurkha fellow-prisoners of Captain Hari Budwhar were
greatly uplifted by this Indian cavalry officer's example.

Among many ordeals Captain Budwhar's most celebrated act of defiance was to have the audacity to survive
suspension for nearly ninety days in a cage in the market
square of Bangkok. Following his release the 2nd Gurkhas
presented the captain with a silver kukri in a gesture which
could not have been more opportune amid India's political
uncertainties after the war. Although the 2nd Gurkhas
could not have appreciated it at the time, Captain
Budwhar's silver kukri was symbolic of changes which were
imminent, among them the appointment of Indian officers
to Gurkha regiments of an independent India.

During the last days in Burma John Masters had
observed, as he noted later, the old Indian Army going
down to the attack for the last time. The Indian Army
which Masters and such other officers from Indian Army
families as General Sir Walter Walker of the 1/8th Gurkhas
had joined between the two world wars was still, for all its
mechanisation, the Indian Army of Kitchener, Roberts and
in some respects of Young who had refused to run away
from Gurkhas in the Nepal War; and of Ochterlony, the
terrible Lony Ochter who had had the good sense to leave
the defeated Gurkhas with their honour, an independent
state and an unoccupied Katmandu.

In 1947 the granting of independence to India and the
division of the subcontinent into the Hindu and Moslem
states of India and Pakistan brought to an end the British
Crown's control of the Indian Army through the Viceroy
and the Commander-in-Chief, India. For Gurkhas Indian
independence involved as decisive a parting of the ways as
was the political separation of India from Pakistan. Not
until a week before the 15 August handover did the Gurkha

regiments know what their fate was to be; how they were
to be apportioned in the inevitable break-up. As Hindus
there was, of course, no possibility that Gurkhas would be
asked to serve in the Pakistan Army, but there was much
trepidation about their future as they awaited the news.
When the order came it placed the 1st, 3rd, 4th, 5th, 8th
and 9th Gurkhas in the army of independent India while
the 2nd, 6th, 7th and 10th passed to the British Army.
While British officers of regiments assigned to India had
no choice but to leave—they were to be Indian-officered—
Gurkhas were not compelled to serve either India or Britain
against their will.

The break-up was symptomatic of general change.
Shortly after the Japanese capitualtion Sir Judha Shamsher,
whose terse 'of course' in the tradition of the formidable
Sir Chandra, had guaranteed 100,000 Gurkhas for service
wherever Britain chose to send them, had retired to spend
his days in spiritual contemplation at Hardwar in India;
and now the Rana dynasty of prime ministers, which had
hitherto reduced the throne to a powerless object of holy
reverence, was itself on the way, yielding to a resumption
of royal rule. The changes in Nepal did not and have not
in the present reign of King Birendra altered the Himalayan
kingdom's traditional welcome to Britain's recruitment of
Gurkhas; nor is there any denial of the needs of India's
regiments, or for that matter of the demand for a body-
guard battalion of Gurkhas by Lee Kwan Yew, the Prime
Minister of Singapore. Far from objecting to Britain's
continued employment of Gurkhas the Government of
Nepal has grown increasingly nervous in recent years that
a contracting British Army might dispense with Gurkhas
altogether; a potential economic blow in terms of British
pay and pensions which contribute so handsomely to the
subsistence of innumerable Nepalese villages.

In 1948, after the regiments had overcome the first
emotional problems of division as between India and

Britain, the four British regiments of the Gurkha Brigade made their headquarters in Malaya where for twelve years they were actively and successfully engaged in a jungle hide-and-seek with subversive Chinese communists.

India also found suitable post-war employment for its Gurkhas, or Gorkhas as it prefers to call them, reverting to the old-time spelling of the Gurkha home, detaching the 3/1st and 2/5th Gorkhas to the United Nations as part of its force in Africa during the Congo troubles. With all their previous frontier experience behind them, the 8th Gorkhas were despatched to patrol the Ladakh region in order to watch for Chinese incursions of this most inhospitable territory. Marching, if such an orderly process can describe the Gurkhas' struggle to move in the face of ferocious blizzards at 18,000 feet to counter a Chinese attack in 1962, the 8th relived the climatic experiences of the Gyantse expedition early in the century.

The valour and endurance of Gurkhas engaged against the probing Chinese on the northern borders of India in the 1960s demonstrated that while they were now serving under Indian or their own officers, they had not lost any of the spirit which sustained them in two world wars. It also serves as a reasonably recent reminder that Professor R. L. Turner's often quoted eulogy from the preface to his *Dictionary of the Nepali Language* still holds good:

As I write these last words my thoughts return to you who were my comrades, the stubborn and indomitable peasants of Nepal. Once more I hear the laughter with which you greeted every hardship. Once more I see you in your bivouac or about your fires, on forced march or in the trenches, now shivering with wet and cold, now scorched by a pitiless and burning sun. Uncomplaining you endure hunger and thirst and wounds, and at last your unwavering lines disappear into the smoke and wrath of battle.

Bravest of the brave, most generous of the generous, never had country more faithful friends than you.

The Gurkha Brigade, serving with the British Army, while losing none of its fighting efficiency, reputation and incomparable jungle-craft as was so evident in the Indonesian troubles of the 1960s, gradually acquired fresh skills which were as necessary to a highly mechanised and automated army as the bravery in action which will carry a man forward in the face of machine-gun fire. They became engineers and operational signallers and were given their own army service corps. But the Gurkha battalions of the British Army, now removed from Malaya to Hong Kong under their new title the Gurkha Field Force, which henceforth is not likely to exceed 6,000 men, remain at their best as rifle battalions, enlisting from the hills of Nepal the 'bravest of the brave'. Given the required ingredients, an advance held up by a machine-gun manned by a determined, possibly fanatical enemy, Gurkhas ever remain in the Victoria Cross class. But of course such opportunities have become rare since, in November 1965, Lance-Corporal Rambahadur Limbu of the 10th, serving in General Walker's Borneo force, charged an Indonesian machine-gun post. Subsequently he received his Victoria Cross at Buckingham Palace from the Queen.

Now, as successive British governments seek economies in the armed forces, it seems likely that in the absence of regular opportunities for conventional warfare the chances for Gurkhas to use their martial skills will continue to decrease. An operation such as the speedy airlift of a battalion of Gurkhas from Britain to protect its sovereign base areas in Cyprus at the time of the 1974 Turkish invasion of the Mediterranean island may never be repeated.

Yet Gurkhas also make excellent ceremonial soldiers and hold an honoured place in British affections. Should it develop that keeping faith with Nepal remains the only reason for recruiting Gurkhas for British service, it is still possible that no British government, however doctrinaire, will declare the Gurkha and his kukri redundant.

APPENDIX 1

Gurkha Regiments of the British-Indian Army

* In British service since 1947 partition of India

THE 1ST KING GEORGE V'S OWN GURKHA RIFLES (the Malaun
Regiment)
Originated in 1815 as the 1st and 2nd Nasiri (Friendly) battalions. 1850, the 66th Bengal Native Infantry; various subtitles
including the Gurkha Light Infantry. 1903, the Malaun Regiment added to title. 1937, the 1st King George V's Own Gurkha
Rifles (the Malaun Regiment) after being the 1st King George's
Own Gurkha Rifles (the Malaun Regiment) since 1910. 1947,
the 1st Gorkha Rifles.

THE 2ND KING EDWARD VII'S OWN GOORKHA RIFLES (the Sirmoor
Rifles)*
Originated as the Sirmoor Battalion raised by Lieutenant
Frederick Young in 1815. Briefly in 1861, the 17th Bengal Native
Infantry, later the 2nd Goorkha Regiment. 1936, the 2nd King
Edward VII's Own Goorkha Rifles (the Sirmoor Rifles) after
being the 2nd King Edward's Own Goorkha Rifles (the Sirmoor
Rifles) since 1906.

THE 3RD QUEEN ALEXANDRA'S OWN GURKHA RIFLES
Raised in 1815 as the Kumaon Battalion. Briefly in 1861, the 18th
Bengal Native Infantry before becoming the 3rd Gurkha
Regiment. 1907, the Third Queen's Own Gurkha Rifles. 1908,
Alexandra added to title. 1947, the 3rd Gorkha Rifles.

THE 4TH PRINCE OF WALES' OWN GURKHA RIFLES

Raised in 1857 as an extra Gurkha Regiment. 1861, briefly the 19th Bengal Native Infantry, then the 4th Gurkha Regiment. 1924, the 4th Prince of Wales' Own Gurkha Rifles. 1947, the 4th Gorkha Rifles.

THE 5TH ROYAL GURKHA RIFLES (Frontier Force)

Raised in 1858 at Abbotabad and known as the Hazara Gurkha Battalion and the 25th Punjab Infantry. Later the 5th Gurkha Regiment. 1921, the 5th Royal Gurkha Rifles (Frontier Force). 1947, the 5th Gorkha Rifles.

THE 6TH GURKHA RIFLES*

Raised in 1817 as the Cuttack Legion. 1828, the Assam Local Light Infantry. 1886, the 42nd Gurkha Light Infantry. 1903, the 6th Gurkha Rifles. Now the 6th Queen Elizabeth's Own Gurkha Rifles.

THE 7TH GURKHA RIFLES*

Raised in 1902 at Thayetmyo, Burma, as the 8th Gurkha Rifles, it became the 7th Gurkha Rifles in 1907. Now the 7th Duke of Edinburgh's Own Gurkha Rifles.

THE 8TH GURKHA RIFLES

The 1st Battalion originated in 1824 in Assam as the Sylhet Local Battalion, becoming the 44th Bengal Native Infantry in 1861, the 44th Gurkha Light Infantry, 1886, and the 8th Gurkha Rifles, 1902. 1947, the 8th Gorkha Rifles.

The 2nd Battalion began as the Assam Sebundy Corps in 1835, becoming the 43rd Bengal Native Infantry in 1861 and the 43rd Gurkha Light Infantry, 1886. 1902, the 7th Gurkha Rifles. 1907, the 2/8th Gurkha Rifles.

THE 9TH GURKHA RIFLES

Raised in 1817 as the Fategarh Levy, it became the 63rd Bengal Native Infantry in 1824, the 9th Bengal Native Infantry in 1861 and the 9th Gurkha Rifles in 1901. 1947, the 9th Gorkha Rifles.

THE 10TH PRINCESS MARY'S OWN GURKHA RIFLES*

Raised in Burma in 1887 as a military police battalion. 1890, the 10th Madras Infantry, later the 10th Regiment (1st Burma Rifles) Madras Infantry. 1903, the 10th Gurkha Rifles, subsequently receiving the present title.

APPENDIX 2

Indian Ranks

The following Indian ranks were used in Gurkha regiments:

HAVILDAR   sergeant
HAVILDAR-MAJOR   sergeant-major
JEMADAR   lieutenant, platoon commander
NAIK   corporal
SUBEDAR   captain, company second in command
SUBEDAR-MAJOR   major, senior Gurkha officer of a battalion

Bibliography

Bolt, David. *Gurkhas* (Weidenfeld & Nicolson, 1967)

Bredin, Brigadier A. E. C. *The Happy Warriors: The Gurkha Soldier in the British Army* (Blackmore Press, 1961)

Calman, W. Y. *Indian Army Uniforms, Infantry* (Morgan-Grampian, 1969)

Calvert, Michael. *Chindits, Long Range Penetration* (Pan/Ballantine, 1973)

——. *Slim* (Pan/Ballantine, 1973)

Collier, Richard. *The Sound of Fury* (Collins, 1963)

East India Company. Papers Respecting the Nepaul War (1824)

Fleming, Peter. *The Siege of Peking* (Hart-Davis, 1959)

——. *Bayonets to Lhasa* (Hart-Davis, 1961)

Heathcote, T. A. *The Indian Army: The Garrison of British Imperial India, 1822–1922* (Newton Abbot: David & Charles, 1974)

Hutchinson, Colonel H. D. *The Campaign in Tirah, 1897–98* (Macmillan, 1898)

Jackson, Major Donovan. *India's Army* (Sampson, Low, 1940)

James, Harold, and Sheil-Small, Denis. *The Gurkhas* (Macdonald, 1965)

Jenkins, L. Hadow. *General Frederick Young* (Routledge, 1923)

Kirby, Maj-General S. W. *The War against Japan*, 5 vols (HMSO, 1958–69)

Leonard, Colonel R. G. *Nepal and the Gurkhas* (HMSO, 1965)

MacMunn, Lieut-General Sir George. *The Martial Races of India* (Sampson, Low, 1932)

Mason, Philip. *A Matter of Honour* (Jonathan Cape, 1974)

Masters, John. *Bugles and a Tiger* (Michael Joseph, 1956)

——. *The Road Past Mandalay* (Michael Joseph, 1961)

Merewether, Lieut-Colonel J. W. B., and Smith, Sir Frederick. *The Indian Corps in France* (John Murray, 1919)

Morris, John. *A Winter in Nepal* (Hart-Davis, 1963)

Northey, Major W. Brook, and Morris, Captain C. J. *The Gurkhas, Their Manners, Customs and Country* (John Lane and Bodley Head, 1928)

Owen, Frank. *The Chindits* (Calcutta: The Statesman Press, 1945)

——. *The Campaign in Burma* (HMSO, 1946)

Pemble, John. *The Invasion of Nepal* (Oxford University Press, 1971)

Pocock, Tom. *Fighting General: The Public and Private Campaigns of General Sir Walter Walker* (Collins, 1973)

Prinsep, Henry T. *History of Military and Political Transactions in India (1812–23)* (John Murray, 1826)

Roberts, Field-Marshal Lord. *Forty-One Years in India: From Subaltern to Commander-in-Chief*, 2 vols (Richard Bentley, 1897)

Slim, Field-Marshal Sir William. *Defeat into Victory* (Cassell, 1956)

Smith, Brigadier E. D. *Britain's Brigade of Gurkhas* (Leo Cooper, 1973)

Tuker, Lieut-General Sir Francis. *Gorkha: The Story of the Gurkhas of Nepal* (Constable, 1957)

Wakeham, Eric. *The Bravest Soldier: Sir Rollo Gillespie, 1766–1814* (Blackwood, 1937)

REGIMENTAL HISTORIES OF THE 1st–10th GURKHA RIFLES

The History of the First King George V's Own Gurkha Rifles (The Malaun Regiment), Brigadier E. V. R. Bellers (Gale & Polden, 1956)

The History of the 2nd King Edward VII's Own Goorkha Rifles (The Sirmoor Rifles), Colonel L. W. Shakespear and Lieut-Colonel G. R. Stevens (Gale & Polden, 1952)

The Regimental History of the 3rd Queen Alexandra's Own Gurkha Rifles (1815–1927), Major-General N. G. Woodyatt (Clowes, 1929); (1929–1953), Brigadier C. N. Barclay (Philip Allan, 1953)

History of the 4th Prince of Wales' Own Gurkha Rifles (1857–1937), Ronald Macdonnell and Marcus Macaulay (Blackwood, 1940); (1938–1948), Colonel J. N. Mackay (Blackwood, 1952)

History of the 5th Royal Gurkha Rifles (Frontier Force) (Gale & Polden, 1956)

The Historical Record of the 6th Gurkha Rifles (1817–1919), Major D. G. J. Ryan, Major G. C. Strahan and Captain J. K. Jones (Gale & Polden, 1925); (1919–1948), Lieut-Colonel H. R. V. Gibbs (Gale & Polden, 1955)

History of the 7th Duke of Edinburgh's Own Gurkha Rifles, Colonel J. N. Mackay (Blackwood, 1962)

History of the 8th Gurkha Rifles, Lieut-Colonel M. J. Huxford (Gale & Polden, 1952)

The 9th Gurkha Rifles (1817–1936), Lieut-Colonel F. S. Poynder (RUSI, 1937); (1937–1947), Lieut-Colonel G. R. Stevens (RUSI, 1953)

Bugle and Kukri, the Story of the 10th Princess Mary's Own Gurkha Rifles, Colonel B. R. Mullaly (Blackwood, 1957)

Index

The symbols WWI and WWII are used where necessary to differentiate between the two world wars.